HOW TO BE A CHAMPION EVERY DAY

HOW
TO BE A
CHAMPION
EVERY DAY

JOE THEISMANN

RADIUS BOOK GROUP
NEW YORK

Distributed by Radius Book Group
A Division of Diversion Publishing Corp.
443 Park Avenue South, Suite 1004
New York, NY 10016
www.RadiusBookGroup.com

For more information, email info@radiusbookgroup.com.

Library of Congress Control Number: 2020900784

First edition: June 2020
Hardcover ISBN: 978-1-63576-712-4
eBook ISBN: 978-1-63576-716-2

Manufactured in the United States of America

10 9 8 7 6 5 4 3 2

Cover photo by Rob Cannon
Cover design by Charles Hames
Interior design by Aubrey Khan, Neuwirth & Associates

To all the men and women and their families
who have made sacrifices for this great country.

I hope in some way, shape, or form . . .
this book honors you.

CONTENTS

"After the final seconds on the scoreboard tick down, the fans may remember a few of your greatest plays. They may remember that amazing play in Super Bowl XVII. But more than anything, they will remember *you*. So decide right now how you want to be remembered. Then live every day like you're playing the final game."

FOREWORD

by George Bodenheimer

JOE THEISMANN HAD IT all. He was a Notre Dame football legend, a National Football League Most Valuable Player, a Super Bowl champion with the Washington Redskins. He was the quarterback and the leader of his team. But one play ended it all. One play. Those of us who saw that Monday Night Football game in 1985 will never forget it. The flea-flicker to John Riggins. The tackle. The snap of Joe's leg. Giants linebacker Lawrence Taylor calling to the sidelines for help, holding his head in distress. Joe was carted off the field, never to play another game. His career was over. "Poor Joe," so many people thought.

Poor Joe? Not on your life!

Theismann was knocked down but not out. He went on to become an entrepreneur, a businessman, a television and radio sports analyst, and a motivational speaker. It turned out that adversity and being forced out of his comfort zone helped him become a better person. Along the way, Joe discovered that the worlds of sports, business, and life are intertwined. The tenets he learned from football—perseverance, work ethic, personal responsibility, motivation, preparation, and the right attitude—lead to success wherever you are, in whatever vocation you choose.

In this book, Joe Theismann shares the wisdom he gained on his journey. He writes about teamwork, of course, but Joe takes it to a higher level by showing us that the road to success is as much about the people we meet along the way as anything else. And this, perhaps, is the most important lesson of all. He underscores the importance of a handshake and looking that person in the eye when you shake their hand. He reminds us of our own humanity, of what we all have in common, to not take anybody for granted, and to appreciate everybody.

I have known Joe for over thirty years, first at ESPN and now in our work together with the V Foundation for Cancer Research. As a matter of fact, Joe was there in 1993 when Coach Valvano gave his memorable speech at the ESPYs and he instinctively jumped up to help Jim off the stage. That's who Joe Theismann is. He's a champion every day. There's something for everybody in this book. So read on and be inspired.

1

OPPORTUNITY

Game- (and Life-) Defining Moments

Make the most of today.
Because these are the glory days.
Not yesterday. Not the last decade. Today.

ON NOVEMBER 18, 1985, I did something I had never done before. The Redskins were in the middle of a lousy season, which meant that I was in the midst of a lousy season, as well. Here I was, a World Champion quarterback and MVP of the entire National Football League. And yet we had lost five of our first ten games of the season.

Something was off—and I knew I had to turn it back on.

We've all had times in life when we need to have a heart-to-heart with ourselves. This was one of those moments. Sitting in the locker room before the game, I thought, *The world is going to be watching me tonight. What am I doing with my life? What's out there for me?*

I realized I was staring a golden opportunity in the face. We were about to take on the New York Giants in a prime-time matchup on *Monday Night Football,* and it was my opportunity to remind the world, as well as myself, what I was really made of. This was my chance to show the world that the Joe Theismann that they loved (and that I loved) was back.

Energy pulsed through my body. I shot up from my locker, excited. I mean, *really* excited. I made my way down the long hallway toward the field. For eleven years, every time I walked down that hallway, I'd smack the Redskins logo right below the exit sign. Usually, I did so without ever uttering a word. That night, however, as I headed out the exit and hit the logo, I said these words aloud:

"Tonight, your life's gonna change, Joe."

I'd never considered myself to be prophetic (I still don't), but that night, I was right about what was to come. At the end of the first quarter, I was 7 for 10 passing, including a touchdown. As I threw the touchdown pass, I thought, *All right! Joey is back.*

At the start of the second quarter, Coach Gibbs called a flea-flicker, which is a trick play designed to fool the defense into thinking that we were going to run the ball instead of pass it. I called for the snap, took the snap turn, and handed the ball to our Hall of Fame running back, John Riggins.

John started toward the line. Just before he got there, he stopped. We wanted to fool the Giants into thinking it was a run, which meant they'd all be up at the line of scrimmage trying to tackle John, leaving our receivers wide open.

John turned around and pitched the ball back to me. I looked down the field, where there should have been a wide-open receiver—Art Monk. He was covered. I looked to my right for my tight end Donnie Warren. He was covered, too.

All of a sudden, I felt pressure coming from my left side. It was Giants linebacker Lawrence Taylor. He grabbed my left shoulder, swung around, and caught my right leg between the knee and the ankle. As all 240 pounds of Taylor came crashing down on top of me, I heard a *pow! pow!* in my left ear. It sounded like two muzzled gunshots.

That was the night that I got "The Hit." Even today, people cringe as they say, "I saw it on TV that night. I will never be able to forget that sound." And, of course, people also ask, "Did it hurt?"

My leg had snapped like a matchstick. I'll give you one guess. Yes, the pain was unbelievable.

But as I lay on the field with an open compound fracture in my lower right leg, I realized what a magnificent machine the human body is. From the knee down, all the feeling was suddenly gone in my right leg. The endorphins had kicked in, and I was no longer in pain.

 Up until that moment, I had been a one-man show called "Joe Theismann: Football Star."

As they carried me to the sidelines, 55,000 people gave me a standing ovation like I had never heard before in my life. It made me realize how selfish I'd been. I was an ego out of control. I thought I was a one-man show. I thought nobody could touch me.

Obviously, that had just been proven otherwise. Bob Goodrich, the ABC Sports producer, said it was the worst injury he had ever witnessed. O. J. Simpson, Joe Namath, and Frank Gifford were up in the booth announcing the game, and Goodrich said to them, "Guys, this is ugly."

The break was so gruesome that Goodrich questioned replaying it. Despite his misgivings, ABC rolled the replay. As the break played again, either Simpson or Namath let out an audible groan on national television, echoing the feelings of millions of viewers across the country.

I was blissfully unaware of any of this. With my endorphins kicked into overdrive, I had no idea of the extent of my injury. As they put me on a stretcher, I saw Harry Carson, the great middle linebacker of the New York Giants, out of the corner of my eye. I stopped the gurney and called out to him, "Harry, I understand you're thinking about retiring."

"Yes, I am, Joe."

"Well, don't, because I'm coming back."

Carson replied, "That may be the case, pal, but it ain't gonna be tonight."

He was right. I wasn't coming back any time soon. Of course, I could never have guessed that "soon" really meant "ever."

It turns out that Joe Theismann the Star wasn't invincible after all.

When the game restarted after my injury, the first play that Coach Gibbs called was a deep bomb down the right sideline— precisely where I was being loaded into the ambulance. At the moment I was being put in the ambulance, Art Monk made a great catch right in front of me on the sidelines. My leg was shattered and my career was possibly over, but it was just business as usual all around me, as if to say, "Hey, big guy, everyone's replaceable."

On the way to the hospital, my leg remained numb. I had yet to really feel the pain of my injury. In fact, as they moved me from the ambulance gurney to the hospital gurney, I glanced down and noticed that the bottom part of my right leg hadn't made it onto the gurney with the rest of my body. Pretty horrific, right? Yet I didn't feel a thing. Instead, I turned to the attendant and calmly asked, "Excuse me, can you pick up the rest of me and put it on here?"

Once I had been taken to the operating room, where they were going to put me back together, I noticed that someone had rolled an old black-and-white TV (along with a coat hanger antenna) to the other side of the glass. I was able to watch the final minutes of the game, and in the fourth quarter, as the last few seconds ticked down, the Giants threw an incomplete pass. I knew the Redskins had won, so I turned to the doctors and said, "Okay, go ahead and do what you gotta do."

I missed a heck of a football game. I missed out on a whole lot of games after that, too, because that break ended my football career for good. To this day, I'll never know why I changed my ritual and added the words that still ring in my ears: "Tonight, your life's gonna change, Joe."

Be careful what you ask for.

Before that night, you'd turn on the TV and hear about how *Theismann leads Redskins.* Turn on the radio, and it was *Theismann leads Redskins.* Look at the newspaper headlines, and it was *Theismann leads Redskins.* I was good, and I knew it. Then *pow!* It was over in an instant.

Since then, my injury has received millions of views on YouTube and is the subject of the first few minutes of the movie *The Blind Side.* Even today, people are kind enough to come up and ask me how I am doing.

Yes, the injury was a defining moment in my life. But that night on the field wasn't my first defining moment. I was once a skinny high school quarterback (5'10", 152 pounds) who *showed everyone what I was really made of* by leading my team through an undefeated season. Then I got to the University of Notre Dame and I was a high school hero-turned-underdog who finally got an opportunity to shine during my sophomore year—and in the end, once again, *I showed everyone what I was really made of.*

Finally, I became an NFL quarterback who started a career as a punt returner, thought I had it all, then lost it all in a single moment.

 All my life, I've felt like I had something to prove. But to whom?

We've all experienced moments that have changed our lives, or moments that have given us a chance to prove our real staying power. At one point or another, we have all felt like we have something to prove. When a great opportunity arises, we believe it is up to us to show the world what we're really made of.

But there comes a time when you have to ask yourself: *What am I really trying to prove?* And more importantly, *Who am I trying to prove it to?*

What's in a Name?

It may appear that I've had a blessed and lucky life—and in many ways I have. However, nothing good comes easily to those with the will to be the best. Of course, it never hurts to have a last name that rhymes with a coveted trophy, either. But there's a story behind that.

During my senior year at the University of Notre Dame, I was a Heisman Trophy candidate. Most people think it is the most *amazing* coincidence that my last name rhymes with Heisman. *It must have been fate*, they say. They'll even ask, "Are you the guy that trophy is named after?" (If the trophy were named after me, I might have actually won it. But that's another story.)

Here's a little secret I want to share with you: Fate had very little to do with it. I actually used to be Joey Theismann—pronounced THEESMAN—from South River, New Jersey. At the beginning of my senior year in college, our public relations director, Roger Valdiserri, had an idea. During the previous season, a reporter had asked Roger if my last name was pronounced like the trophy. Everyone had a good laugh. But then Roger realized maybe it wasn't so funny.

Maybe it was genius.

One day, Roger called me into his office and asked, "Joe, how do you pronounce your last name?"

A little surprised, I replied, "It's pronounced ThEEsmann."

He shot back, "No, it's not. It's ThEIsmann [pronounced *thighs-man*]."

Again, I said, "No, it's ThEEsmann."

This time, he repeated it more slowly and deliberately. "It's ThEIsmann."

More than a little confused at where Roger was going with this discussion, I said, "Please hand me the phone, Roger. We'll get this straightened out."

I called my dad back home in New Jersey to set the record straight. Any time I ever had a question for my father, he'd always say, "Fire away, Son." I got my dad on the phone and said, "Hi, Pop. I got a question for you."

"Fire away, Joey."

"Dad, tell me. How do you pronounce our last name?"

There was dead silence on the line. Then my dad finally spoke up. "Son, you really do have a problem, don't you? You're a senior in college, and you don't know who you are. What have you been doing for the last three years?"

"Dad, that's not it. Please, just tell me. How do you pronounce our last name? I'll explain later."

He said, "Of course, it's THEESMANN."

"Thanks, Pop," I said. I hung up the phone and whipped around to face Mr. Valdiserri. "Look, my last name is pronounced THEES-MANN. I think my dad knows how to say his own last name."

Roger smiled. "Joe, you don't get it. There's a trophy out there called the Heisman Trophy. It goes to the best college football player in the country. We think you have a chance to win it, but we're not just going to bank on your athletic ability. Nor are we going to count on the reputation of the University of Notre Dame. But we think that by changing the pronunciation of your last name from ThEEsmann to ThEIsmann, to rhyme with Heisman, we can get you that trophy."

That, my friends, is how I wound up becoming Joe ThEIsmann—yes, like Heisman.

Looking back on that time, I recognize that it was the beginning of branding "Joe ThEIsmann." And that's why I shared the story. All of us—and our brands—started somewhere. It's irrelevant where the adventure has taken you or where you are today. You had to start somewhere.

I didn't win the Heisman, but the name and the brand stuck. In fact, five years after my name was changed, as I sat with my mom and dad around the dinner table, I turned to my dad and said, "Pop, I got a question for you."

In his own indomitable way, my dad said, "Fire away, Joey."

"Dad, tell me, how do you pronounce our last name?"

He said, "It's ThEIsmann."

Opportunities in Disguise

In the big picture, tweaking the pronunciation of my name was a pretty small change to make. Whether change is big or small, it is never easy. In fact, people often view change as a liability. This is why an unbelievable 75 percent of change initiatives fail in today's business world.

 Are you really opposed to change? Or are you merely opposed to *being* changed?

It really boils down to perspective: *People aren't opposed to changing; they are opposed to being changed.* But embracing change doesn't mean you have to alter who you are at your core. It means that you are able to take things that are changing around you and use them to your benefit—much like how my name change became a permanent part of my brand. I'm even able to use the story of my career-ending leg break to show others how to embrace life's surprising, and often painful, changes.

Maybe you're thinking to yourself, "Change? No thanks. You can't change me." If you are, I will say this:

If you can't imagine it, you can't achieve it.

Do you know that, at 482 feet, the Great Pyramid of Giza was the tallest man-made construction in the world for almost 4,000 years? How did they do it? To this day, no one is absolutely certain. But the way I see it, it doesn't matter how they did it. What's impressive is that they even imagined they could do it—and then they actually did. This willingness to imagine something and achieve it can also be seen in the young quarterback for the Baltimore Ravens, Lamar Jackson. After an outstanding rookie year in 2018, he wanted to focus on becoming a better passer so he sought to revisit the fundamentals. He widened his stance when he stepped into his throws and also worked on rotating his right hip, creating a more fluid delivery. The results were dramatic. In 2018, his completion percentage was 58.2 percent, whereas in 2019, his completion percentage increased to 66.1 percent. The specific modifications weren't big changes, nor were they necessarily easy, but he wanted to improve at his craft. He put in the time, which resulted in his being voted to the Pro Bowl in 2019 and winning the 2019 NFL MVP unanimously.

It's easy to let change convince us that something is too hard, or even impossible. But we have to be willing to learn something new every day.

I know I can't *make* you successful. This book is not the "quarterback's secret playbook" for success. But regardless of where you are today, you and I have shared some of the same struggles. And my hope is that by sharing the lessons I've learned, you'll benefit from them, too.

I believe that everybody has tremendous knowledge to share. We're all so different—and that's one of the greatest things about life. As the amazing Joel Osteen says, "God did not create us to be average." You are not here to be ordinary; you are filled with immense potential. You have the capacity for *change*.

The word "potential" can be a double-edged sword in football. It often means that a player *could* be great, but he's not playing as he should. In fact, some of the best players are content to sit on the sidelines with their potential neatly tucked away under their uniforms.

It's time to untuck your potential.

 The Bonus Section at the end of each chapter will emphasize how to turn "opportunity" into "competitive edge."

Life is about *opportunity*—which happens to be one of my favorite words. Every morning, you have the choice to tap into your talent and capabilities. Each day, when I am faced with whatever opportunity comes my way, I try to step outside what's comfortable and experience something new—and maybe even something great. When I was in broadcasting, I had the good fortune to be exposed to a variety of people in the football organizations I covered from owners to coaches, players, and equipment and medical staff. I had played for one team my entire twelve-year career; now I had the opportunity to see how thirty-one other teams did it. I learned what the good ones did and what the bad ones were doing. It gave me a foundation to teach the fans and viewers as well as to continue to learn more about the game I love.

Another example is easily seen when the two teams meet in the Super Bowl. They both have the opportunity to be crowned the champion. One will seize the day and the other will be just one of the other thirty-one teams that fell short of hoisting the trophy.

Recognizing opportunities is so important that I have included a bonus section at the end of each chapter to highlight a special story either from my life or about another champion. These stories illustrate how to take every opportunity that comes your way and turn it into the competitive edge you need, whether it's in sports, business, or life.

We all need to prove that we can reach as high as we want to reach in this lifetime. Well, who are we really trying to prove it to? After years of searching for that answer, I finally know that I wasn't trying to prove myself to my coaches. I wasn't even trying to prove myself to my parents or to my fans. I had to prove I was better than the man I was yesterday. Do this *every day* and imagine the person you'll be tomorrow.

The great NFL linebacker Mike Singletary once said, "Do you know what my favorite part of the game is? The *opportunity* to play." It took me a lifetime to embrace the fact that it's not about my ego or what I can prove to someone else. Those defining moments may be what shape us. But some of life's greatest moments will pass right by you unless you are ready and willing to take the sacks you get, along with the triumphs, and turn them into *opportunities*. If you can do that, it will impact your business, your family, and your life in a lasting and positive way.

My vision for this book—and really for the rest of my life—is to take my experiences and use them to help others become champions in their own lives. When you are inspired, feel free to make notes in the book, highlight passages, and add your own thoughts. My wish is that you can use this information to dig deeper into who you are and find out what you're really made of, and that you'll do it first and foremost for *you*.

Then the world will have no choice but to notice.

BONUS #1

A One-Week Commitment =
A Lifetime of Payoff

WHEN I WAS RECRUITED to play football at the University of
Notre Dame, I was one of thirteen quarterbacks on the roster.
That's a serious amount of competition. At 152 pounds soaking
wet, I knew I wouldn't be the obvious pick for starting quarterback. So I decided to create an *opportunity*—a competitive edge—
for myself. I moved to campus a week early, before anybody else
got there. During that week, I sat with the coaches and learned
where to stand in the huddle, I studied the cadence, and I ab-
sorbed the key plays.

I knew that just as bosses in the business world like their meetings to run smoothly, coaches like their practices to run smoothly,
as well. I also knew that coaches would prefer a quarterback who
made their day just a little bit better by helping to facilitate a
smoothly run practice.

To me, the opportunity to stand out and show the coaches that I was ready to learn and help in any way I could was worth far more than the one-week investment of my time and energy.

When the rest of the team showed up a week later for the first practice, no one else knew exactly what the coaches wanted—but I did. Guess what happened? I became the starting freshman quarterback. I wasn't the biggest. I wasn't the fastest. I wasn't the strongest. But I had created an opportunity to show the coaches what I could do and how hard I was willing to work. And it paid off.

I don't care if you're a freshman or the starting quarterback and an All-American Heisman Trophy candidate. If you don't know how the coaches run their practices, you're missing the edge that you need to stand out from the competition when other talented players come vying for your spot. It doesn't matter if you're an entry-level employee or the boss who's calling the shots. If you look around you, there are a million opportunities waiting to be created. And those opportunities will give you the competitive edge you need to be where you want to be in life.

"Where you wind up in life is a direct result of how you see yourself getting there."

2

ATTITUDE
Be Your #1 Fan

Before you can win,
you have to believe you will win.

THERE ARE SONGS IN everyone's life that hold special significance. I bet there's a special tune that always reminds you of your childhood and brings a smile to your face. And there's probably a song that teleports you back in time to high school or to your first date, and maybe even one that transports you back to the day you met your significant other. Songs can also have the power to ignite a competitive mindset: During practice and before games, my teammates and I listened to music to get ourselves pumped up and ready to take on the world.

I may not be suiting up to face my opponents on a football field anymore, but I still appreciate and respect the influence of music. For me, there are few songs more powerful and meaningful than Tim McGraw's "Live Like You Were Dying." The song is about a conversation that Tim had with a man who had been told he only had a few months left to live.

This song is one of Tim McGraw's greatest hits. It was co-written by Craig Wiseman and Tim Nichols; in *Nashville Songwriter*, author Jake Brown recounts the story of how the song came to exist. A mutual friend of Wiseman and Nichols—a young man and a new father—went to the doctor for a routine exam. Much to the young man's surprise, the doctor walked into the room and broke the news to him that there was an unusual mass visible on his X-ray.

The young man was immediately panic-stricken. He started to examine his life and what was left of it—which he thought was very little. A few weeks later, the mass turned out to be nothing more than a nonthreatening genetic defect. Nevertheless, when Wiseman and Nichols heard that story, their creative wheels started turning.

Wiseman and Nichols talked to their friends and family members who had received their own "death scares" and asked them what their reactions were after their diagnoses. Wiseman's uncle, when told by his doctor that he had leukemia, retired on the spot and went shark diving. Nichols recalled a story about a woman whose cancer diagnosis compelled her to drop everything and go mountain climbing in the Rockies. Before they knew it, the idea of "living like you were dying" was born.

You can take "Live Like You Were Dying" for what it is—a catchy country melody with an interesting backstory. Or you can choose to take those words to heart, as I have done. Let me ask you this: If your doctor said to you, "I'm so sorry, you only have six months left to live," would you continue to live your life the exact same way you are living it today? Or would you live it differently? If your answer is, "I'd live it differently," then my next question is:

What are you waiting for?

Why wait until your time is almost up to start living your best life? Why go through the motions and let your circumstances control you, rather than calling the shots *yourself?* When you live life on someone else's terms, you are allowing fear to take the reins. *Fear* is what tells you that a big goal is "too risky." Fear is what whispers in your ear, "Everyone will laugh at you when you fail, so why bother?" Fear is *not* your friend—fear is a poor counselor and is known for giving the world's worst advice. Stop listening to fear and start listening to what *you* want to get out of life.

Life is a lot shorter than we realize. Whether you've got six months or six decades left on this earth, make the most of every minute. You cannot hug your kids enough times or tell your significant other that you love him or her enough. You should spend whatever time you have on this earth doing all your favorite things—as well as a few things that scare you.

If you've been going through the motions until now, that's okay. We've all been there. But here's the great news: You can decide to change right here and now. You can choose to "live like you were dying" by adjusting just one thing: *your attitude.*

Attitude Precedes Everything

Attitude precedes absolutely everything we do. It affects and ultimately determines how we approach relationships, our jobs, and how we wake up in the morning. Every *response*, every *action*, and every *reaction* is determined by our attitude.

Perhaps even more significantly, attitude also determines outcomes. Have you ever noticed how people who believe they are destined to fail almost certainly *do* fail? On the other hand, people who believe they can win almost certainly *do* win. In many ways, that makes the right attitude even more important than skill, talent, or knowledge.

Marty Schottenheimer coached four teams—the Cleveland Browns, Kansas City Chiefs, Washington Redskins, and San Diego Chargers—and suffered through only two losing seasons in twenty-one years as an NFL head coach. In the locker room before the games, he would tell his players:

I want you to *think* about winning.

I want you to *talk* about winning.

And I want you to *expect* to win.

Thanks to this pep talk, Schottenheimer's players competed with a ferocity that was palpable from the stands. He knew how to fire them up, and he knew how to get their attitudes right. In turn, his players demanded the same energy from the fans who cheered them on. Marty's attitude became contagious, spreading to thousands of people week after week. Most of us could only dream of having that kind of positive effect on others!

Former Kansas City Chiefs wide receiver Danan Hughes, who played under Schottenheimer for six seasons, said this about his coach in a 2013 ESPN article, "Marty Schottenheimer Coaching Tree: Motivator, Consistent Winner Produced a Multitude of Successful Head Coaches":

He could take players like myself [a seventh-round pick] or undrafted guys and get the most out of us . . . Marty literally could brainwash players into thinking they were more than they were.

Now that's the power of attitude. As Marty used to tell his players, it's imperative for us to *think* about being successful, to *talk* about being successful, and to have an *expectation* of success. And if we use that same frame of mind for the way we approach life, it will give us the greatest chance of reaching our goals and fulfilling our vision.

Then, when I started speaking professionally, I noticed that the most popular speaking topics in the corporate world were the exact same subjects that were popular in football. People in the business world talk a lot about goals and customer service—which is really just about people and relationships. They also talk about teamwork and motivation. But the most important topic in business and in sports is attitude. Having the right attitude leads to success. Like professional athletes, successful business professionals inherently know that attitude determines how far you go—for an organization, an individual, or a team.

Displaying the right attitude and expecting success are not optional for those of us who want to win. It's important to be supported by others and to have people who believe in you—but all the support in the world can't help someone who doesn't expect to win. Why should someone else think more of you than you think of yourself? You should be your #1 fan!

It's all about attitude.

Dave Liniger, the founder of the real estate giant RE/MAX, once said, "If I could buy you for what you *think* you're worth and sell you for what I *know* you're worth, I'd be a rich man." You should consider yourself priceless. You should believe that *no one* could afford you. When you start to see yourself in that light, you'll discover that the right attitude forms the framework for becoming a champion.

The Essence of a Champion's Attitude

Want to change where you are in life? Change the way you *look* at life. It really is that simple.

Notice that I didn't say *easy*. "Simple" isn't always easy, but I've discovered a little secret over the years: *Life is going to turn out exactly how you think it will.* When things happen that weren't a part of the plan, that doesn't mean that your positive attitude didn't work. Life isn't that vindictive; that's just the unpredictable nature of human beings. We aren't promised tomorrow, or even the next few seconds. Every moment is a gift. That's not a cliché—it's the plain and simple truth.

On March 4, 1993, I was blessed to witness something that will stay with me forever. I was attending the ESPY Awards, where Jimmy Valvano was being honored with the inaugural Arthur Ashe Courage Award.

Jimmy V first made headlines in 1983 when, against all odds, his North Carolina State Wolfpack won the NCAA Championship against the Houston Cougars. It was one of those thrilling, iconic moments in sports history. When the clock ran out and Jimmy realized his team had won, he raced up and down the court in disbelief, looking for someone to hug. He was a great coach, and an even better man.

On this particular night in 1993, when he was being honored with the Arthur Ashe Courage Award, he had made it to the awards ceremony despite the fact that he was fighting a losing battle with a very aggressive type of cancer. When asked about that night in a 2013 *Huffington Post* article ("Jimmy V Speech: Valvano Delivered Inspirational ESPY Remarks While Battling Cancer"), Dick Vitale, the famed college basketball broadcaster and a close friend of Jimmy's, said, "I remember how sick Jimmy was that evening. I honestly did not know how he was going to make it up to the stage, and I remember standing next to him, in total awe as he spoke. We helped him off of the stage that evening, and he was absolutely amazing in his words as he talked about beating cancer."

I was standing there with Dick as we helped him onto the stage. Despite his failing health, Jimmy spoke for more than ten minutes about his life and his illness with a positivity and perspective that continues to inspire others to this day. In fact, I carry a copy of his life-changing speech with me wherever I go. I want to share a portion of it with you now, because his words have shaped everything I do and talk about when it comes to attitude:

To me, there are three things we all should do every day. We should do this every day of our lives. Number one is *laugh*.

You should laugh every day. Number two is *think*. You should spend some time in thought. Number three is, you should have your *emotions moved to tears*, could be happiness or joy. But think about it. If you laugh, you think, and you cry, that's a full day. That's a heck of a day. You do that seven days a week, you're going to have something special.

Just a few weeks after that memorable night at the ESPY Awards, Jimmy passed away at the age of forty-seven—a young age to be taken, by anyone's account. Even so, when people remember Jimmy V, no one dwells on the sadness of his passing—instead, people remember the positivity of his life. His attitude was too powerful even for death to overcome.

Jimmy himself said it best: "Cancer can take away all my physical abilities. But it cannot touch my mind, and it cannot touch my heart, and it cannot touch my soul. And those three things are going to carry on forever."

In his closing remarks, Jimmy told the audience about the new charity he had just founded with ESPN called The V Foundation for Cancer Research. He then recited their motto: *Don't give up, don't ever give up*, before adding, "And that's what I'm going to try to do every minute that I have left."

Life is not about the struggles. It's about the journey itself and the legacy you leave behind, which reflects the kind of life you led and the attitude you conveyed. So consider adopting the same kind of attitude that Jimmy had, whether you've got a little or a lot of time left on this earth.

Dancing in the End Zones of Life

People often give wide receivers a hard time for celebrating in the end zone after a touchdown. I admit, I've seen it get a little out of hand (that is, when it was a touchdown for the opposing team). But when you really stop and think about it, when was the last time you congratulated yourself? People don't take the time to congratulate themselves for their victories, big *or* small. They think that giving themselves a pat or two on the back will brand them as an egotist in the minds of others.

 Displaying confidence in your abilities is not about ego. It's about conviction.

But liking and accepting yourself doesn't mean that you are an egotist. Attitude has to grow from a place of sincerity, which means that you have to believe, deep down, that you are good enough and smart enough to get where you want to go in this life. It's not about ego—it's about conviction.

Parents are full of wisdom, and my mother was no exception. In fact, my mother shared so many nuggets of wisdom with me over the years that I've given them a name—I call them "Mom-isms." It's one thing to listen to our parents; it's another thing to really *hear* what they are saying. When your parents try to share a "teaching moment" with you, it's important to remember that they are doing so with the best of intentions. So cherish your parents, love them, and appreciate them, because when they're gone, you can't pick up the phone and ask any more questions or seek their advice.

I say this because I've lost both my mother and my father. I know all too well the feeling of needing my parents' wisdom, and then experiencing that sting that inevitably comes with the realization that their wellspring of insight is gone.

I'm truly grateful for all the knowledge I was blessed to receive from my mother and father, and I fondly remember and often recall their words. Especially those "Mom-isms." Here is one of my favorites:

Mom-ism: "Joey, the only way that you're ever going to be able to like other people is when you like who you are and are satisfied with who you are as a person."

I didn't know it at the time, but when my mother said those words, she was speaking a profound truth. Through her wisdom, I came to realize that it really is okay to congratulate yourself. In fact, it's beneficial to start your day doing so. It's a lot better than the way many people start their day. Tell me if this scenario sounds familiar:

Crawl out of bed with a groan. Mutter something under your breath about needing to get a better alarm clock that isn't so annoying. Stumble into the bathroom. Turn on the light. Look in the mirror and gasp in horror at the reflection glaring back at you. Moan, "Oh, my hair," or "Look at those bags under my eyes," or "Geez, I'm so out of shape."

If that sounds familiar, you are not alone. But here's a far better way to start the day:

Wake up and greet the day. Walk into the bathroom, turn on the light, look in the mirror, and tell the person looking back at you, "Hey, you! You're lookin' good. Go out and have a terrific day. Make this day a special one."

You think that's too cheesy? I understand. Some things are simply out of our comfort zones, and people aren't always ready to step out of those zones. *But* . . . when you get tired of having another mediocre day, try it, and see what a difference it makes. I bet you'll find that a little excitement about life makes a huge difference in how you live it. If you want to change where you are in life, you must change the amount of energy you put into it. Life equals energy.

Enthusiasm Precedes Success

It's time to get excited about life and greet the day with words of congratulations and encouragement—because life is literally *fueled* by our enthusiasm. We all start out in this world with a high level of excitement, but somewhere along the way, we lose our childlike passion—you know, the kind of joy we used to feel at Christmas or when we finally learned to tie our own shoes. For many people, at some point in adulthood, the fire of enthusiasm just seems to burn out.

In those rare instances when you *do* come across someone who has that spark of enthusiasm still burning, you can't help but stop and take notice. One example of such a person is Hall of Fame quarterback Brett Favre. As great a quarterback as Brett was, one of the most outstanding things about him was his passion and enthusiasm for the game. He could carry out a "pump fake" (pretend he was about to throw, but not actually release the ball) better than anybody in football, and when he successfully fooled the defense into reacting to the fake throw, he'd jump around like a little kid in celebration.

Another prime example is quarterback Tom Brady. When the Seattle Seahawks threw the interception at the end of Super Bowl XLIX, Tom Brady leaped into the air on the sidelines, more excited than a boy who just met Santa Claus for the first time. Both Brett Favre and Tom Brady displayed an attitude of enthusiasm and a level of excitement that is quite simply infectious.

You don't need anyone's permission to get excited. Life itself is reason enough! You woke up this morning, right? That wasn't a guarantee, so go ahead, take a moment and get excited about it. If you begin your day with a negative attitude, you don't stand a chance. Choose the right attitude and choose to be excited.

Why do you think the Green Bay Packers love to play at Lambeau Field? Why do you think I loved playing at RFK Stadium when I played for the Redskins? Why do you think the Denver Broncos love their home games at Mile High Stadium? Why do you think the Cubs like to play at Wrigley Field? The excitement of their own hometown fans cheering them on makes playing the game that much sweeter.

 ### Be the kind of person who brings enthusiasm and energy into every room you enter.

Enthusiasm doesn't just affect *you* and *your* day. It affects everyone around you—your partner, your kids, your co-workers, and everyone else you come into contact with along the way.

Have you ever felt someone enter the room? I mean, really *felt* someone's presence come into a room? Some people have a tangible excitement that follows them like a shadow. Over the years, I have repeatedly noticed this phenomenon in the speaking business. When certain emcees or executives step onstage, the room starts humming with excitement. On the other hand, if someone walks onstage with no energy and no passion, it sets a downbeat tone for the entire meeting.

A quote that's often wrongly attributed to Ralph Waldo Emerson sums up the importance of enthusiasm best: "Enthusiasm is one of the most powerful engines of success. When you do a thing, do it with a will, do it with your might, put your whole soul into it, stamp it with your own personality. Be active, be energetic, be enthusiastic and faithful, and you will accomplish your object. Nothing great was ever achieved without enthusiasm."

As with the best things in life, moderation is key. When it comes to congratulating yourself, you have to walk that fine line between confidence and arrogance. I learned where that line was the hard way—and more than a few times. One of those lessons came in Toronto, Canada, a number of years ago. I was the keynote speaker to an audience of 3,000 at a fancy black tie dinner. I have to admit, I was feeling mighty important sitting there in my tuxedo at the head table.

At one point in the evening, the waiters brought out the entrées, along with baked potatoes and baskets of bread. I had just helped myself to some dinner rolls when I noticed that I had only been given a single tab of butter—*one* lonely tab of butter for my rolls and a baked potato. Now, I'm decent in the area of management, but I'm not that good. I spread the single tab of butter on my potato, and then I turned to the young man standing behind me and said, "Excuse me, son, I'd like another tab of butter."

His reply came swiftly. "No."

That was not the response I had expected to hear. "Now, wait a second. See all these people? They've come here to see me. I'm Joe Theismann, and I'd like another tab of butter, please."

Undaunted, the boy replied, "Sir, I know who you are. You are a great football player."

I said, "Thank you very much."

He said, "You are an MVP in the NFL."

I said, "Thank you very much."

He said, "You won a Super Bowl."

I said, "Thank you very much."

He said, "But, sir, do you know who I am?"

I stopped. "No, I don't."

He replied, "I'm the kid in charge of the butter. You get one tab of butter."

Talk about a moment that brings your feet back down to earth. It was a humbling experience, to say the least. But the message I received from that young man was right on the money: There is not a single one of us who is more important than the person sitting next to us, regardless of title or station in life.

Every now and then, life has a way of putting us in check. And we need it. Otherwise, all the congratulations we give ourselves and receive from others will breed a sense of entitlement.

My leg break was one of those "life just put me in check" moments. When I got hurt, I became extremely introspective, and it led me to this realization: Sometimes other people put us back in line, and sometimes we do it for ourselves. And if I had to choose between the two, I'd prefer to take myself back down to earth rather than wait for life to do it for me.

Confidence Shapes Attitude

One of the building blocks of a winning attitude is that healthy level of confidence that we've been discussing. This confidence develops when you allow yourself to feel good about your successes and remain optimistic that there are more successes waiting for you down the line. To *believe* that you can accomplish something is so important. But how does one create this self-confidence?

It's not always easy. And in my experience, today's younger generations especially struggle with it. I see so much talent in the up-and-coming faces I meet, but many of them don't believe in themselves—they don't have that inherent feeling that says, "I can do this. I can accomplish this. I can meet this challenge."

Believing that you can do something
is far more than half the battle.
It's most of the battle.

Boy, I've been there. I bet we *all* have at some point in our lives or our careers. When I got hurt and lost my status as a star football player, my confidence was shaken to its core. For a moment, I wasn't sure there was anything left to feel confident about if my name wasn't stamped on the back of a jersey. But when I stepped back and examined my life, I realized where my source of confidence was rooted—and I believe it's the same for all of us. It comes from performing four specific actions in life.

1. Anticipate Your Success

The most confident people anticipate winning. When it comes to anticipation, I am always reminded of Hall of Fame coach Bill Walsh. He was a good friend and someone I was privileged to play for in a Pro Bowl. Walsh formulated what has become popularly known as the "West Coast Offense" during his time as assistant coach for the Cincinnati Bengals from 1968 to 1975. (Walsh later went on to make his mark as the head coach of the San Francisco 49ers from 1979 to 1988.) The West Coast Offense is an offense that is characterized by short, horizontal passing routes—instead of running plays—to "stretch out" the defenses of the opposing team, all to create the potential for long runs or long passes. Through the popularization of this offense, Bill Walsh forever changed the way the game of football is played.

One day, Coach Walsh was telling me how he used to videotape all of his offensive installation meetings. The purpose of an offensive installation meeting is to give the offensive players a chance to learn precisely how they are going to handle all the game situations, and this is done by walking through each scenario in a slow, thorough manner. It allows the offensive players to see how each group (offense, defense, special teams) functions as a whole, and how the chosen scheme or strategy applies to game situations.

It's important to point out that teams always change certain parts of their offense and defense each season—it's actually a yearly ritual in the NFL. So, why bother taping it if it's going to be modified? When I asked Coach Walsh this question, he replied, "Joe, it's because I'm going to anticipate that we're gonna be successful. And in anticipating our success, I know that our offensive coordinators are gonna go on and become head coaches of their own teams. And I don't want to lose the fundamental teachings of our system."

Coach Walsh also filmed the meetings so that future offensive coordinators (OCs) would have the right foundation to teach offensive players what it took to win. He believed that his offensive installations would be successful, and he believed his coaching staff would be successful. By taping the meetings, he was anticipating the success of both his offense and his coaches.

His anticipation certainly paid off. If you need proof, take a look at the 49ers' record under Bill Walsh. They were a true dynasty in the eighties—and I believe that was due, in large part, to Coach Walsh anticipating their success.

Sun Tzu, the ancient Chinese warrior and philosopher, eloquently summed up the power of anticipating success more than two thousand years ago with these words:

"Win the war, then fight the war."

I was anticipating my success long before I even realized that's what I was doing. Before I joined the NFL, I played three seasons of football in the Canadian Football League for the Toronto Argonauts. After a solid rookie season in 1971, I started the 1972 season with high hopes. But at the beginning of the season, I broke my leg. It was nothing like "the break," but it was certainly enough to put me out for most of the season.

As I sat at home waiting to heal, I decided to put my time to good use. I wasn't happy with my signature, because I didn't believe it was the kind of autograph that would look good on a football. So I took out a marker and started creating an all-new signature for myself on footballs, hoping that someday someone would think I was good enough to want my autograph on a ball. In that moment, even though I didn't realize it yet, I was performing an action that indicated my belief in myself. I was anticipating that, one day, people would *want* my autograph. In other words, I was anticipating my success. My new signature was a start to another Joe Theismann, who would go on to sign a lot of autographs.

2. Be an Insatiable Learner

When it comes to building confidence, there is no better building block than knowledge. When I was a kid, I couldn't care less about reading and studying. Today, I'm an avid reader. I can't get enough. I want to learn as much as I can about everything I can—not just about sports. I read about music; I read about art; I read about business; and I read a lot about finance, which is my passion. I enjoy trading equities, working in the world of economics and finance, and learning how companies operate behind the scenes. So much of my time today is consumed by growing and educating myself in any way I can.

People who think they already know everything there is to know about their line of work or their industry are missing an opportunity to grow and reach their true potential. Here's a quick assignment for you. Find a highlighter and highlight the following line: *How much do I know about my business? Can I learn more?*

Be honest and truthful in your response. It's one thing to study your competition. But being willing to study and learn about yourself can give you a competitive edge. You'll find that when you open yourself up to the possibility that you don't, in fact, know *everything*, you will discover a wealth of knowledge that will boost your confidence and strengthen your championship status.

3. Be a Tenacious Worker

Another element of confidence is hard work. It's one thing to *want* to do something. It's another to actually *do* it—to invest the blood, sweat, and tears necessary to bring an idea, goal, or vision to fruition.

Thomas J. Watson, the founder of IBM, once said this: "You work the first eight hours of the day for survival, and everything after that is an investment in your future." The winners in this world aren't afraid to put in the work and put in the time. I've seen it over and over again in the NFL—the players who work the hardest are the best. That's a cold, hard fact.

Back when I was in broadcasting, we were at an Arizona Cardinals practice, and I was on the sidelines waiting to interview a future Hall of Fame receiver, Larry Fitzgerald. I had to linger on the sidelines for quite some time after the team finished for the day because Fitzgerald "had" to catch at least fifty more footballs. (Keep in mind this was *after* a grueling two-hour practice.) But those fifty extra catches? *That's* what made Fitzgerald one of the best receivers.

Becoming successful, truthfully, is not that difficult. Some people luck into success; other people are willing to do what it takes to get to the top; and some people work hard enough to reach a target they've set for themselves. Those are all great accomplishments, but I will say this:

Anyone can become successful.

Staying successful is the true challenge.

Obtaining success is no small achievement, but maintaining it is the greatest challenge. And the only way you can do it is by putting in the work.

4. Show Up Prepared

Muhammad Ali wasn't just one of the greatest athletes of all time. He was also a master of words. Here's one of my favorite quotes of his: "I hated every minute of training, but I said, 'Don't quit. Suffer now and live the rest of your life as a champion.'" How true those words are. Before you walk out onto the field, before you make your presentation at the company's big annual meeting, or before you walk into that sales presentation, take the time to prepare to be a champion.

All of the previous actions I've mentioned—anticipating, learning, and working hard—boil down to one thing: preparation. If you want the enthusiasm . . . that leads to the confidence . . . that leads to the right attitude . . . that leads to the actions . . . that lead you to the top and keeps you there, you must *prepare* to be successful.

When I played football, I spent countless hours going over my game plan, taking notes in meetings, and studying film. I spent far more time preparing than was required by my coaches, because that was the degree of preparation I felt I needed in order to succeed.

When I got into broadcasting, I took that same attitude about preparation. About a week before I was scheduled to announce a game, I started reading every article I could get my hands on about both teams. I would travel to the game location on the Thursday before a Sunday night game and spend all day Friday with the home team, talking to players and coaches, watching practice, and studying film. On Saturday, we would meet with the visiting team's players and coaches and look at more film. On Sunday morning, we would have our TV production meeting and go over our game plan for the upcoming game.

By the time the game started, I'd put in over sixty hours of preparation. That included taking all the information I'd gathered and putting it on a "spotting board" that I would place in front of me during the game. It had players' names, stats, where they went to school, and what we had talked about in production meetings. It also included what the coaches had shared with us. I never wanted to leave anything to chance. If it was a great game, I would probably use only 25 percent of what was on my board—but if it was a blowout, I'd use about 75 percent. I never knew how the game was going to go, so I always wanted to be as prepared as possible.

Stepping Outside the Comfort Zone

On September 29, 1985, we played the Chicago Bears at Soldier Field in Chicago, Illinois. For those of you too young to remember, 1985 was the year that the Chicago Bears had one of the greatest seasons in all of sports history. They captured the nation's attention by nearly nailing an undefeated season and doing it with swaggering flair. They were a true force to be reckoned with and awe-inspiring to watch.

And yet somehow, early in our game against the Bears, we had a ten-point lead. Needless to say, we were feeling pretty darned excited about it. We were trying our best to keep the ball away from dangerous Bears wide receiver and kick returner Willie Gault—the fastest man in football—and so far, we'd kept the kickoff successfully out of his hands three times. Unfortunately, the next kickoff landed in Willie's arms and off he went. He ran. And ran. Before we knew it, Willie ran ninety-nine yards to score the Bears' first (and not their last) touchdown of the night.

It was the beginning of the end for the Skins. On that play, our punter, Jeff Hayes, tore his thigh muscle, and he was down for the count. With no backup punter, Coach Gibbs knew we were in trouble. But I had a brilliant idea. I thought to myself, *What a great opportunity! I can step in and punt. How hard can it be? You drop the ball, you raise your foot, and* BOOM. *I can do that.*

I walked up to Coach Gibbs. "Coach, you're looking for a punter?"

He said, "Yeah, Joe. I don't know what we're gonna do."

I said, "I can punt."

Coach said, "You can what?"

I said it again. "I can punt."

Coach shrugged. "Fine. Next time we punt, you punt."

We went back out on the field and got the ball on our own thirteen-yard line. Then we ran a running play and gained two yards to inch up to the fifteen-yard line.

It was second down and eight. I looked to the sidelines at Coach Gibbs. He wanted me to throw. *Okay,* I thought. *This is going to turn into a great opportunity for me.* I dropped back and picked out a kid in the third row. *Bam!* Into the stands. *Aw, darn. Shucks, it's incomplete.* I didn't want to mess up my punting opportunity by getting a first down.

Now it was third down and eight. Coach wanted me to throw again. With no open receiver, I threw it toward the ground to avoid an interception. *Okay, fourth down. Time to show the world that Joe Theismann can throw and kick. After all, the quarterback of the Dallas Cowboys, Danny White, was both a quarterback and a punter. Why couldn't I be that, too?*

The offense ran off the field and on ran the kicking team. As we lined up, my teammates kept yelling, "Kick the ball right, Joe. Kick it right."

No problem, I thought. I called for the snap. Then, as the ball hit my hand, it was as if the world started moving in slow motion. I kept reminding myself, *Kick the ball right, Joe. Kick it right.* I looked down at the ball, dropped it, and watched it go firing off my foot. *Pow!*

Well, maybe not *pow*! It was more like . . . *ker-plop*.

What happened after that wasn't pretty—the ball went thirty yards sideways and sixteen yards forward, which meant that it went a total of *one yard* past the line of scrimmage. *One. Yard.* Can you believe it? It might as well have gone backward.

After the punt (if you can call it that), my guys were running around looking for the ball. I didn't want to admit that I'd seen it go flying over the Bears' bench on the sidelines. In the aftermath of the "shank heard 'round the world," six Bears rushed up to me and congratulated me with, "Way to go, Joe! We can't wait for you to kick again!"

The game went on, despite my attempt to remind everyone that, as Mike Ditka later put it, "Joe Theismann doesn't get paid to punt." The Bears scored yet again, and we got the ball back. I ran up to Coach Gibbs and asked, "Coach, what play do you want to run next?"

He looked down at his play sheet. "I want spread right, short motion, sixty outside."

"Great!" I said. Then I added, starting to chuckle, "And, Coach, do you want me to punt again?"

He gazed at me with utter shock in his eyes. Then, slowly and very deliberately, he pushed his glasses up his nose and looked me square in the face before emphatically uttering these words: "I never want to hear the word '*punt*' coming out of your mouth again."

As you might have guessed, that was my last punt of the game. In fact, it was the last punt of my career. That colossal shank meant I had a one-yard average in my career as a punter in the NFL, and I actually retired from football holding the record for the second shortest net punt in the history of the game. Sean Landeta of the New York Giants holds the record for the shortest net punt in the history of the NFL—and, ironically, it just so happens that his "record-breaking punt" was on the same spot in Soldier Field where my one-yard effort took place. (As for Sean's punt, he says the wind got ahold of the ball that day, and that he "barely ticked it.")

We lost to the Bears 45–10 that day. It was a slaughter. Even today, when people kid with me about our ill-fated game at Soldier Field against the unconquerable force that was the '85 Bears, they'll say things like, "Oh, Theismann, you sure were a failure as a punter."

But I don't see it that way. I wasn't a failure—I just had an educational experience that didn't go my way. Sometimes things don't go the way we plan. I know that. You know that. What I learned that day was that I'm not a punter, but when the team needed me to help, I wasn't afraid to try. Does that mean we should never try anything for fear of failing? Of course not. Look for the good in people and situations and expect to find it. In fact, here is another *Mom-ism* for you:

Mom-ism: "If you go looking for the bad in people, you're probably going to find it. If you go looking for the good in people, you're probably going to find that, too."

I'd like you to try a few simple exercises with me to test your comfort zone boundaries: Try eating with your opposite hand or crossing your legs differently. Fold your arms comfortably and naturally, the way you always fold them. Now uncross your arms and fold them with the other arm in front. It's uncomfortable, right? I bet it feels a little strange. Do you know why? It's because you aren't used to doing it. You're doing something that is outside your comfort zone.

Nothing truly worth achieving in life is going to be attainable without getting a little uncomfortable. Don't be afraid to step outside the box and try something new, even if you might not be good at it. That's how I choose to approach life.

To me, life is a cup half full, not half empty, which means there is an opportunity hidden behind even the seemingly bleakest of circumstances. Don't be afraid to try something different. When you become willing to try new things, that's the moment when fear stops controlling your life.

 The right attitude allows you to find an opportunity hidden in the bleakest of circumstances.

I love the game of golf, but there is a certain par-three at TPC Sawgrass in Jacksonville, Florida, that makes me a little nervous. It's the seventeenth hole of The Stadium Course that features the famed "island green." Most people approach that hole thinking, *I know I'm going to lose some balls in the water. The real question is, how many balls?*

The greatest golfers walk up to the tee with *one* ball in hand because they *believe* they can hit the green. They don't need the safety net that a pocketful of balls provides. That's the crucial difference between champions and everyone else, whether in sports or in life: World Champions don't see the hazards; they just see the path to the green.

Whether or not you are a pro golfer, the way you approach a hole like that has a lot to do with your attitude. It can also tell you a lot about how you approach life itself. *Do you see the green as opposed to the hazards?* If you don't, now is the time to step up to that tee with just one ball. Don't focus on all the hazards—don't focus on all the ways you could fail.

It will feel uncomfortable at first, and you may be tempted to retreat back to familiar ground. However, once you remove all of your go-to "safety nets" in life, you will begin to trust yourself more than ever, which will breed incredible confidence, as well as results.

"Why Not?" or "Why Me?"

A quote that's often attributed to Stephen Hawking (but is actually much older) states, "Intelligence is the ability to adapt to change." That's quite a comment coming from one of the most brilliant minds in history. But he's right, of course. More than your academic studies or your IQ, your *willingness to adapt* to the changes around you is a critical component of successfully stepping outside your comfort zone and embracing the deviations that come from doing so.

Stepping outside your comfort zone is one thing—it's something you can elect to do if you so choose. *Change* is another thing altogether. Change just *happens*, whether you want it to or not. You may not see it coming, but once it comes, you have to be willing to embrace that change. Here's why, in the words of John C. Maxwell: "Change is inevitable. Growth is optional."

In 1985, when I got hurt, I was forced to deal with some serious and sudden change in my life. I went from being a professional football player to a man looking to survive. I became a man searching for a way to transform who he was, what he was, and the way he looked at life. And I realized that I had to change my attitude in order for the transformation to be successful. If I changed my attitude, I would grow; if I didn't, I would fade away under the shadow of my former glory.

In times like that, when we are staring in the face of unexpected change, it's tempting to say, "Why me?" That mindset is dangerous, as it forms the groundwork for a victim's mentality.

Champions don't say, "Why me?" They say, "Why not?"

Think of the changes you experience every day—at work, in your family, and throughout your life. If you approach them by saying "Why not?" you are choosing to face them with optimism, hope, and an expectation that there's nothing this world can throw at you that you can't handle.

In 2002, I had the unique opportunity to present an award to a young man named Neil Parry. Neil, a safety from San Jose State University, had been selected to receive the inaugural New Orleans Bowl Inspirational Award—and what an inspiration he was. Neil walked onto the San Jose State University football team in the fall of 1999 not knowing if he would make the team. In the end, he didn't just make the team; he got to play as a freshman. After a successful first season and a good start to his sophomore season, Neil's life was about to change.

On October 14, 2000, during the third quarter against their conference rival UTEP (University of Texas at El Paso), Neil was chasing down a kick returner on special teams when another player was knocked into the front of his right leg. The result of that freak accident was a compound fracture of the tibia and fibula that broke through the skin. Neil and I had the same exact injury—but with one crucial difference. After three days in the hospital, Neil developed a deadly temperature of 105 degrees. That's when the medical staff discovered that his leg had become infected. Neil now feared for his life.

Nine days after the injury, doctors informed him that they were going to have to amputate his injured leg below the knee. That would be devastating news to anyone, but it's especially catastrophic to someone who dreams of playing professional football his entire life. Yet in a press conference just one month after the amputation, Neil made an announcement that took everyone by surprise. He announced that he was determined to play NCAA football again.

As Elliot Almond chronicled for the *San Jose Mercury News*, Neil told the crowd of stunned fans and reporters that he had developed a motto—NGU, or Never Give Up—that would keep him motivated to achieve his goal of playing again. It certainly seemed to work. He underwent twenty-two surgeries and went through numerous prosthetics with the goal of returning to the game.

On September 18, 2003, Neil walked back onto the field as a member of the punt return team. He went on to play in eight games that season, gain national attention, and he even met Presidents Bill Clinton and George W. Bush.

When most people would have cried, "Why me?" Neil said, "Why not?" His attitude was such that he was not going to allow any setback—even an amputated leg—deter him from getting back on that football field. It just wasn't going to happen. And it turns out he was right.

Throw Out the Playbook

Here's a story that epitomizes the enormous potential that comes from stepping outside your comfort zone from time to time. A lot of you may have heard of the former Carolina Panthers' head coach and now the current head coach of the Washington Redskins, Ron Rivera. What many of you may not know is that Ron Rivera—or "Riverboat Ron" as he is affectionately called—is an unlikely source of inspiration in the area of taking chances.

Ron is a "checklist" kind of guy. For example, he's got a checklist of thirty-two items that he goes through before every single game prior to going out on the field. He's calculated, and he has always relied heavily on analytics when it comes to how he calls plays.

But one day, Ron experienced a *revelation*, the kind of epiphany that can only come from a heart-beating, chest-pounding moment in life. It was 2013, and his Panthers were 0–2 for the season. They were about to play the New York Giants. While driving near his Charlotte-area home, he was consumed by his decision not to "go for it" on a late-game fourth and one in a one-point loss to the Buffalo Bills the previous week. (He had chosen the "safe" option of attempting a field goal.)

In fact, he was so preoccupied that he never saw the traffic light turn from green to red.

"I got so focused in on that decision, I ran a red light and almost got sideswiped," Rivera told Jim Corbett of *USA Today*. "After that I'm like, 'What was I thinking?' And I realized that these are the things I have to do to give us a chance to win."

The "things" that Ron was referring to were *chances*. He realized that he needed to gamble a little if he wanted the really big payoffs—hence his new moniker, "Riverboat Ron," named after the riverboat casinos. That didn't mean he was going to start throwing out the playbook or stop relying on analytics and statistics. He simply saw the big picture a little differently from that point on.

"Life, like a career, can be over in a flash," he said. (I'm living proof of that.) "Sometimes you need to take a chance, to lose your inhibitions. Be yourself and not what some imaginary book says you should be. I finally figured out what I had been doing was going by the book."

In 2012, the Panthers lost three games going by the book on tough fourth-down calls. In 2013, after Ron's awakening, they went for it nine different times on fourth downs—and made it on eight of them. In other words, he took some chances, even though gambling is not in his nature. And if you ask Ron about his new nickname, he'll insist that he is not a gambler—he is merely "a calculated risk taker."

The outcome of taking those chances speaks for itself. After Ron stepped outside his comfort zone and made calls that scared him, the Carolina Panthers gained tremendous confidence, set a club-record eight-game winning streak, and secured their first winning season and playoff appearance in five years. In fact, they did it all with a schedule that NFL.com ranked as the "strongest in the league" that year.

There's no doubt that the 2013 Carolina Panthers had some amazing talent on the roster. However, I also believe a lot of their success had to do with Riverboat Ron's moment of revelation, after which he started approaching life with a "why not?" attitude and started taking bold chances.

Your attitude really does determine where you will go—and there are some particularly special words that sum up my sentiments on attitude more than anything else. They come from a poem called "Attitude" by Charles R. Swindoll, a well-known preacher and prolific author.

As Swindoll so eloquently puts it, your *reactions* to life are what define your life—not the hand you are dealt, not the people in your life, and not your situation. If you want something badly enough, no circumstance can stand in your way.

I started this chapter with a song, and so it seems fitting that I end it with a song, as well. I have always loved Whitney Houston's "One Moment in Time." In the song, the late, great Ms. Houston talked about the almost indescribable feeling of experiencing that one great moment that you have always dreamed of.

I was blessed to be a part of a World Champion football team and to be a part of "one moment in time" at Super Bowl XVII. I was truly fortunate to have played with a bunch of guys who believed we could get it done. We weren't the biggest, and we weren't the fastest, but in 1982, we truly believed we could go all the way. Our attitude was such that nobody was going to stop us but us. It was that kind of attitude that allowed the 1982 Redskins to be successful. It enabled us to enjoy a single moment in time that until then was something we had only dreamed about.

I know there is that one moment you dream about, too—the moment when you will say to yourself, *"This is it. This is what I've been working for. This is what it's all about."* Whatever big moment you are dreaming of, let that be the moment that continues to shape your attitude, day in and day out.

As Ms. Houston sang, "The answers are all up to me." Attaining that moment is completely within your control, and your attitude is ultimately what determines whether you experience that moment (or moments) in your own life. I certainly hope you do—because there's no other feeling that can compare to the feeling of realizing an extraordinary goal or dream.

Tell yourself you *can* and you *will.*

Then work hard to prove yourself right.

BONUS #2

Finish Mowing the Grass

A COMPETITIVE EDGE CAN be gained in many different ways. You can seek out opportunities in life to stand out. You can work harder than everyone else. You can even want it more than anyone else. However, championship-level results won't come until you cease one particular activity. If you're like most people, you probably have an assortment of projects—both at work and at home—that are partially complete. Some are halfway done, some 20 percent, some 80 percent. People generally attribute this phenomenon to procrastination—but I prefer to see it as a lack of focus.

Here's an example from my own life. One day, I was mowing the grass at my ranch. As I was riding along on my tractor, I noticed that one of the fence posts on the edge of the property had fallen over. I was only halfway through mowing, but I jumped off the tractor to investigate the fallen post. I decided to fix it while I was thinking about it.

In the middle of digging a new hole for the fence post, I noticed that there was a bunch of brush growing over the fence. I had only dug a partial hole in the ground for the post, but I left the hole to investigate the weeds. I decided to clip the overgrowth while I was thinking about it.

By then, it had gotten dark. And it suddenly occurred to me that the day was over and I had accomplished the following: *I mowed half the grass, I dug a partial hole for one fence post, and I cut a small portion of some weeds.*

The next morning, I felt an unmistakable feeling—dread. Normally, I would have awakened excited to go work on my ranch. But that morning, I had to start the day off by completing three unfinished projects from the day before.

These days, you won't find many unfinished projects lying around my ranch. That feeling of anxiety about facing all those incomplete tasks is not a sensation I want to voluntarily invite back into my life.

People ask me all the time, "How do you manage to fit in all the things you do—traveling to speaking engagements, making guest appearances, managing your restaurant, spending time with family, cutting grass, playing golf, and taking time for yourself?"

It boils down to two things: time management and focus. When you start five projects and bounce back and forth between each rather than tackle one project at a time, you rob yourself of momentum. You also waste far more time than you realize. On the other hand, when you finish one thing before moving on to the next, you feel like you accomplished something. You gain both traction and confidence, and you can lay your head down at night feeling good about what you achieved that day.

Focus is such a simple and mighty tool that has made a powerful difference in the way I manage my time. It is yet another way to help you gain the competitive edge you need to succeed.

Starting a project and not completing it is like marching all the way down the field and not scoring.

"You don't win a Super Bowl by merely becoming successful. You win by staying successful until the fourth quarter ends."

3

GOALS
A Champion's Greatest Ally on and off the Field

Don't let what's happening on the outside
affect the kind of person you are on the inside.

I Didn't Break My Leg

It's been three decades since my leg snapped in half on national television. And yet even today, people approach me with a wince of pain in their expressions and tell me how sorry they are that I broke my leg. I sincerely appreciate the condolences, and I always thank them for their concern. Sometimes the unexpected happens. It was out of my control. The next and most important thing was how I was going to handle it.

It's a small but important difference.

In the smallest moments, in the blink of an eye, your life can change forever. I want to take a moment to demonstrate just what I mean. I want you to snap your fingers right now. *Snap!* That's how quickly your life can change. That's exactly what happened to me on November 18, 1985. At 10:04 p.m., I was the starting quarterback for the Washington Redskins. At approximately

10:05 p.m., two bones in my leg were instantly shattered—and so was my career.

Back when I was in training camp, a reporter once asked me how long I wanted to play the game of football. I replied, "Until they carry me off the field."

I guess I'm more prophetic than I thought.

IT SEEMS LIKE NO matter how hard we try to "prepare for the worst but hope for the best" or anticipate the "bumps in the road," when something unexpected or traumatic happens in our lives, we're never truly ready. It's not like I was able to go on a farewell tour to all of my favorite stadiums, say "thank you" to the fans, and receive an engraved gold watch. There was no warning. No farewell tour. No gold watch. No two weeks' notice. It was just . . . over.

The physical challenge I faced after my horrific injury was difficult, but the mental challenge was even greater. All of my life, whenever I achieved success—whether it was in high school, at the University of Notre Dame, or in the NFL—people were constantly patting me on the back and congratulating me for being so talented and terrific. I had become dependent on that praise—that validation—and then all of a sudden, it was gone.

After I was released from the hospital, I went back to Redskins Park, and for a single moment, it felt like I had never left. But when I walked into the locker room, that feeling quickly vanished. As I looked around, it felt like I had never even been there at all. And then came a real punch in the gut: I found that Steve Bartkowski, the former quarterback of the Atlanta Falcons, had been signed and had already moved all of his belongings into *my* locker. I was a part of the past.

As I walked away on crutches and entered the equipment room, I found my entire career—all eleven years of it—in a box. There was my bloody chinstrap, pictures of my family, keepsakes that people had given me over the years, my clothes, my shoes, and other personal items. Everything I *thought* I was fit into one measly box on the equipment room floor.

When you've lived your whole life as an athlete, and then you're suddenly unable to do the things you love and are admired for, it's the loneliest feeling in the world. At 10:04 p.m., I had been such a vital part of a team. At 10:05 p.m., I had become a pariah, an exile, and an unwanted intruder in a club where I was no longer welcome. From that point forward, my former teammates smiled and said hello to me, but we didn't exist in the same world anymore. Our bond was forever broken. An entire team of guys who had been my friends quickly became cordial acquaintances.

Everything I thought I was had been stuffed into a cardboard box on the floor of the equipment room.

Starting Over (Without Starting Over)

If you've ever lost your job or experienced any kind of unexpected change, you know exactly the feeling I've been talking about. We've all experienced feelings of loss and disconnection at some point in our lives. The first time I ever felt that isolation was the period of painful recovery after my leg break. For at least six months, I struggled with getting my head around what was happening in my life.

In 1984, I had signed a new contract worth over $5 million. Now the contract was gone, and I faced a financial dilemma. *What am I going to do to pay the mortgage?* I also faced a physical dilemma. *Will I be able to do the things I want to do with my life?* On top of that, I also faced a mental dilemma. *Where do I go? And who am I without football?*

I wrestled with these questions for months. And then one day the answer hit me like a ton of bricks. Vince Lombardi once said, "Football is like life—it requires perseverance, self-denial, hard work, sacrifice, dedication, and respect for authority." Boy, was he right. I had learned a lot through my success as the quarterback of the Washington Redskins, as well as from winning a Super Bowl, being the MVP, and being named Man of the Year. Just because I couldn't play football anymore didn't mean that I had to start over from scratch.

I wasn't going to let all of those years on the field go to waste. I wasn't going to hang up my cleats and forget that it ever happened. I already understood the price I needed to pay to be special, and I also knew that I needed to become a better person than I had been. I had truly been blindsided, and not just on the field that night. I had been blind to my own status as a human being. I could no longer be that guy who was so mesmerized by his own glory that he couldn't see those around him.

Thankfully, I still had my restaurant to fall back on. But up until then, I had not been involved in the day-to-day operations. If I had a prayer of succeeding, I needed to learn how to apply what I had learned on the field to the world of business. And I needed to do it quickly.

I also realized that I needed to look outside myself and seek answers from those around me. During my football career, I had recognized the need to learn from those who had *been there, done that.* If there really is "nothing new under the sun," then why should I reinvent the wheel when someone else already has? That's why I tell folks all the time:

If you want to learn to do something well, talk to people who already do it well.

I'll never forget the conversation I had years ago with a young man who was a running back. He was ecstatic after completing a training session with Jerry Rice, the greatest wide receiver in the history of football. As I was talking to this young man about his training regimen, he exclaimed, "Joe, I'm so excited! I got to train with Jerry Rice."

I smiled. "I bet you are excited! Remind me again, what position do *you* play?"

 Why start from scratch? I've learned a lifetime of lessons *on* the field that can be directly applied to life *off* the field.

He said, "I'm a running back."

"Well, Jerry Rice is a wide receiver," I reminded him. "Maybe I could help facilitate a conversation with Walter Payton. Walter does what you do—he's a running back. You see, offensive linemen train differently than wide receivers do. Quarterbacks train differently than running backs do. The training regimen at the pro level is different for each position. Why not talk to a guy who does what you do? With great respect for Jerry and his work ethic, he's a wide receiver. If you want to be a champion running back, go find out how the champion running backs train."

That same lesson applies to you and me right now. It doesn't matter what profession you're in; someone out there has been successful at it and knows how you can be successful, too.

But during times of change in your life, as you look around yourself for answers, you must also look within yourself, like I did. Reflect on your past successes and ask yourself: *"How can I do it again?"*

During my time of reflection after my career as a professional athlete was over, I stood at a crossroads in my life, not sure which direction to take. That refection helped me recognize that I could take the lessons I'd learned from the field and apply the same principles to my new sphere outside the stadium.

The first place I started applying what I had learned—and I believe everyone needs to start here, too—was in the area of goal setting. It doesn't matter who you are or what you do; you need goals. And your goals need to be an active and powerful force in your daily life.

A Vision Is a Goal with a Playbook

People like to lump the terms *dream, vision,* and *goal* together, as in, "My goals are my dreams," or "My vision and my goal is to be better at my job." In reality, each word has a specific meaning. We will talk about how to set SMART goals momentarily, but first I need to make an important distinction.

When we talk about vision, it has to be more than what we see with our eyes. It is what we see for ourselves on life's journey, the purpose we want our life to have, the people whose lives we want to be a part of, and dealing with those unexpected circumstances that we sometimes view as setbacks when they are actually blessings. A vision isn't something you write down and check off a list. It's about what we can do for others rather than for ourselves.

My vision is to take my past experiences—both the good and the bad—and share them with others as a speaker, motivator, and coach in order to change lives and impact people in a positive and lasting way.

Let's say you are a talented leader, builder, entrepreneur, writer, athlete, coach, or teacher. That talent is a gift. And unless you use your gift for the good of others, it's a gift wasted.

Two of the gifts that I was given were my athletic skills and the opportunity to accomplish certain achievements in the world of sports. But all of that was just the setting of the table; that wasn't the meal. At the time, I *thought* it was the meal, and it felt like performing for the glory, the fame, and the money was enough. Now I see that it was preparing me to be able to help other people achieve their dreams, reach their goals, and find their visions that will impact others.

As we move forward with our discussion of goals, keep your supreme vision in mind. Decide what your gift (or gifts) are and articulate a vision that allows others to benefit from those gifts. If you do that first, setting goals and keeping them will be a whole lot more attainable.

A Goal Is More Than a Dream

We've talked about the difference between a goal and a vision. It's also important to point out that *goals* are not the same as *dreams*. Dreams come from the heart. You may not write down your dreams, but you certainly write down your goals. *In fact, if you don't write it down, it's not a goal.* An unwritten goal is really just a way to ensure eventual disappointment down the road.

Walk into any locker room—from the WNBA to the NFL to the NCAA. It doesn't matter where you go. You'll see goals posted in locker rooms for all to see.

The best coaches take their team goal-setting seriously. All coaches require it: The goals are not merely suggestions. For example, Coach Gibbs of the Redskins broke each game down piece by piece so that we'd end up with twelve specific goals that we had to accomplish each time we took the field. There were offensive goals, defensive goals, and special teams goals. These goals were written down and posted.

This strategy is also effective outside the world of sports. If you ask any of the world's most successful businesspeople and entrepreneurs, they'll tell you that writing down your goals is not optional. *It's imperative.*

When you write down your goals, you can see them every day and regain focus on how to reach those goals, just as my teammates and I used to do before and after every practice and every game. Companies hold annual meetings for this exact reason. Annual meetings, quarterly reviews, and the like are meant to establish concrete goals as a group for the next year, often quarter by quarter. The best athletes and the most successful businesspeople know that goals get results.

If you ask the people around you whether they think it's a good idea to write down their goals, I guarantee you that every last one of them will say, "Oh sure, yeah." Yet I once read an article that reported that as many as 95 percent of the people living in this country "refuse" to write down their goals.

 The old adage "out of sight, out of mind" is never truer than when it comes to goals.

The word "refuse" really jumped out at me. Why would anyone refuse to write down a goal? When people reject the practice of goal-setting, it's usually not because they are lazy or can't be bothered to take the time to write their goals down. In reality, the reasons boil down to this: *If you keep your goals in your head, they're easy to change, revise, and eventually ignore.* In other words, "out of sight, out of mind" rings oh so true when it comes to goals. In addition to that, not writing down goals allows you to evade accountability and gives you the "benefit" of not having to face failure if you don't reach your goals. But by avoiding the possibility of failure, you're also avoiding the possibility of great success. When I reinvented my signature, I was actually writing down a goal.

In sports, everyone agrees that it makes sense to set visual targets and aim for them. In business, we expect the companies we work for to have goals for us to hit, such as sales targets and quotas.

So when it comes to figuring out your own personal goals, many people think, *I can do that.* Feeling confident, they pick up a pen and get out a sheet of paper—only to stare at that blank sheet of paper until they grow frustrated and give up.

The thought of seeing your goals taped to the mirror every morning may make you nervous for a number of reasons. I get it—I've been there, too. Setting the number of touchdown passes I wanted to throw in a game? No problem. Picking up a pen and writing down my *personal, professional, spiritual,* and *financial* goals? Not so easy.

It may not have been easy, but I did it, still do it, and will continue to write down my goals for as long as I'm on this earth. I figure it's better than the alternative, which is to become a rudderless ship, allowing the currents of life to do the navigating for me. A lot of people seem to be content with this method of going through their lives. They may drop anchor here or there, but they aren't actually the ones steering the ship.

That's no way to live.

What do you really want out of life? You'll be amazed to find that once you decide where you want to go—and once you set goals to help you get there—your life has more meaning, and things start to move in the direction *you* choose. When *you* call the plays in your own life, your vision becomes the wind that blows the sails.

Setting Goals Like a Champion

I always say that the harder you chase something, the more difficult it is to accomplish. We aren't chasing dreams here; we are creating a realistic game plan for achievement. Champion quarterback Peyton Manning once said, "Pressure is something you feel when you don't know what the hell you're doing." Without written goals, everything—and I mean *everything*—becomes harder and more nerve-wracking than it should be.

What kinds of goals get results? There is a popular goal-setting acronym that has always worked well for me. It's all about setting and writing down SMART goals:

SMART =
Specific. Measurable. Attainable. Realistic. Timely.

Specific

Goals need to be specific. How specific do you need to be? Take this goal: *I want to be a good person.* That's a nice thought, but it doesn't answer the question, "What do I really want in life?" It's too vague—and the words *vague* and *goal* don't get along well together. But how about this goal: *I'd like to be vice president of sales.* That's more specific, and there are real steps that you can take to get there.

 What do you really want in life? If you want it, then say it aloud, claim it, write it down, and be specific!

Let me tell you about a time I set a very specific goal. I was a freshman at the University of Notre Dame, and it was the first day of practice. I looked around and there I was, surrounded by brawn and muscle.

I had gotten there a week early in an attempt to gain a competitive edge any way I could, but I knew I had to do more to ensure my future on the team. At the time, the University of Notre Dame was known for recruiting great athletes who played the quarterback position and then were turned into something else, like a wide receiver, a running back, or even a linebacker. But they couldn't turn *me* into anything else—I was just a quarterback with a decent arm. So when I got back to my room after the first practice, I sat down at my desk, took out a piece of paper, and wrote the following:

"I will be the greatest quarterback that ever played at Notre Dame."

I knew that anyone who saw that sheet of paper—and then saw me—would think I was nuts. But I didn't care. I put that goal into the physical realm by writing it down, and I believe that the act of writing it down was a defining moment in my life.

Another defining moment in my life came in 1968 during my sophomore year at Notre Dame. On the roster was quarterback Terry Hanratty, a Heisman Trophy candidate; Coley O'Brien, who had won a National Championship; and Bob Belden, another great senior player. Then there was Joey Theismann, sophomore quarterback (and remember, at the time, I was still Joey THEESMAN).

Right after the seventh game of the season against Navy, Terry Hanratty hurt his knee during practice. Our coach, the legendary Ara Parseghian, had a few choices. He could have gone with O'Brien. He could have gone with Belden. But he didn't. He turned to me and he said, "You're in. You're the starting quarterback."

That was the turning point in my college football career. I ended up playing twenty-five games as the starting quarterback for the Fighting Irish with a 20–3–2 record. I also set records at the University of Notre Dame that took many years to beat. And then there was the record I set for "most yards passing in a game." That game was in 1970 against our historic rivals, the University of Southern California. We were playing in a torrential rainstorm, and at the beginning of the second half, Coach Parseghian turned to me and said, "Look, Joe, we're basically going to have to throw every down." We couldn't run and it actually was easier to throw in that weather. Wide receivers knew where they were going and defensive backs had difficulty covering them.

I knew I could handle a wet football so you may as well have handed me a winning lottery ticket. Quarterbacks can only dream of being able—and actually being expected—to throw every play. *This could be one of the greatest things that ever happened!* I thought. I threw for 527 yards in a blinding deluge, but sadly, we still lost the game. It was a bittersweet moment.

When I first arrived at the University of Notre Dame, I didn't know what the results were going to be. But when I wrote down my goal, I opened up the doors of possibility and created the opportunity.

Whether or not I became the greatest quarterback that ever played at Notre Dame is insignificant. It was something I believed in and wanted and worked hard to achieve. I may never truly know what caused Coach Parseghian to choose me to start that game my sophomore year, but I do know that I had already imagined it. I had put it out there as a *specific* reality that I could and would attain. I was making my own path, and ultimately choosing my own direction.

Measurable

You've decided on a specific goal; that's a great first step. Now it needs to be measurable. How about this for a goal: *I want to be rich.* While it's good to want to make more money, provide for your family, and be able to give to charity, goals have to be measurable. This means that you must establish concrete criteria for measuring your progress. When you have a way to measure your progress, it makes it easier to stay on track and reach your target by a projected date. Once you experience the excitement of achieving a goal, that will spur you on to setting and achieving even more goals down the line. For example, something as simple as cleaning up your desk. Don't just write down "clean up desk." Write down "clean up desk today."

Athletes know that *momentum* plays a critical role in their success. A "winning streak" leads to more wins because of the momentum each win creates. Players run faster, jump higher, and perform better with the right amount of momentum. Give yourself the momentum you need by setting measurable goals. To determine if your goals are measurable, ask yourself questions like, "How long will it take me to achieve this goal?" and "How will I know when it is accomplished?"

 SMART goals give you the momentum you need to create your own "winning streak" in life.

Attainable

Now that you have figured out a specific, measurable goal, it would be a tragedy not to achieve it, wouldn't it? That's why the next step is so important. Once you've identified your goals, you need to figure out the ways to make them come true. When you see the way to the finish line, that's when you start to develop the attitudes, skills, abilities, and financial capacity to get there. You can also begin to identify some of your previously overlooked opportunities and even discover ways to reach your goal faster.

You can attain almost any goal you set when you plan your steps wisely and make sure that each of those steps is within your reach. When you use this step-by-step approach to goal setting, goals that may have seemed out of reach eventually move closer and become attainable—not because your goals shrink, but because you grow and expand to meet them.

When you physically list your goals, you build up your self-image. You see yourself as worthy of those goals, and you develop the traits and personality that allow you to achieve them. Additionally, once you start hitting some of the benchmarks you've set for yourself, you'll gain positive reinforcement from others around you. And that will get you even closer to the next step—or to the completion— of your goal.

Realistic

In order for it to be realistic, a goal must represent an objective toward which you are both *willing* and *able* to work. A goal can be both high and realistic. And *you* are the only one who can decide just how high your goal should be. What does an unrealistic goal look like? It differs for everyone. You have to factor in your physical or financial situation, then take it one day at a time. For example, you want to lose weight. That's realistic, but how much and in what time frame is so important.

Setting a realistic goal is not the same thing as aiming low. Strangely enough, a high goal is often easier to reach than a low one because a low goal exerts low motivational force, which in turn creates less of the momentum that you need to keep going. The key is to be sure that every goal represents substantial progress—and that it is progress that you can track. Shoot for the moon, and if you fall a little short, you will still land among the stars. And that's not a bad place to be.

Timely

The right goals are grounded with a time frame. With no time frame tied to something, there's no sense of urgency. "Someday" won't work. I suggest forming a time frame of one to five years and deciding what you would like to accomplish personally, professionally, spiritually, and financially within that window, year by year.

If you want to lose thirty pounds, when do you want to lose it by? If you want to get a big promotion, by when do you want to achieve it? If you anchor your goal within a time frame, like "by December 1" or "by June of next year," then you've set your unconscious mind into motion to begin working on the goal.

But just like in football, be prepared to "call an audible" with your goals. When you write your goals down, they aren't written in stone. Your goals are places you want to go in life and things you want to accomplish. However, the circumstances of life may change those goals along the way.

It's comparable to what your life looks like before and after marriage and family. When you're single, your goals reflect the priorities of one person—yourself. When you get married and have a baby, all of a sudden, *wow*! The game has changed. Now it's all about providing for your family, making sure they have a roof over their heads, and ensuring your children grow up in the right environment. As life goes on, you modify and change with the ebbs and flows—and so should your goals.

The Power of Your Mind's Eye

There's one key aspect to making this whole process worthwhile, rewarding, and meaningful. Written goals work because they are *visual*. By seeing something, by making it physical, we make it real.

When we were practicing to play in Super Bowl XVII, I would always get my ankles taped by our trainer, Bubba Tyer, before heading out to the field. The entire time Bubba was taping my ankles, I'd be staring at the wall behind his head. Why? He had placed pictures of the sixteen previous Super Bowl rings right there on the wall. There it was, in the physical universe. That's what I was playing for. It was what we were all playing for—that big, shiny ring. The visualization made it feel both real and attainable.

Our small fraternity of thirty-three quarterbacks who have been fortunate enough to win World Championships and earn one of those rings knows that, in part, it comes down to visualization. It is a vital part of getting to where you want to be in life. If you see it, you can accomplish it. But first you have to be able to see your goal in *your mind's eye*—only then can you take it a step further by articulating the path to get there. In other words, you can't say, "I want this promotion more than anything!" and then sit back and expect the universe to get you there.

Josh Beckett was a Major League pitcher who played for the Florida Marlins, the Boston Red Sox, and the Los Angeles Dodgers. During a conversation I had with him, he told me that when he was playing, he used to have the letters AVE written on the inside of his cap. Those letters stood for *analyze, visualize,* and *execute.* His career was filled with major victories, and it's clear to me just how important visualization was to his success.

 Hope is not a strategy.

"Wanting" and "wishing" aren't skills that are listed on the resumés of champions. You have to write your goal down and then figure out what price you are willing to pay to achieve it. Write down the plan and keep it at the forefront of what you do each day. Stop "wanting" it so bad and stop chasing dreams. Do you know that the harder we chase something, the further it runs away from us? It's always going to be beyond your grasp until you decide to let whatever it is come to you—and goals give you a pathway to get there.

What's Your Price?

Goals won't work without a little sacrifice. Goals won't work without a little sweat. No pain, no gain, right? What price are you willing to pay to be special? We're not talking about the price you are willing to pay to be average.

For me, when it comes to the price I am willing to pay to achieve my goals, the answer has always been, "Whatever it takes." Coach Gibbs had become head coach of the Washington Redskins in 1981, and so far, we were 0 and 5 for the season. He didn't draft me—he inherited me. I wasn't *his* quarterback. And after the season we were having, I had a feeling that he was seriously considering benching me and finding his own guy who could get the job done. I knew that when you inherited a position, you had to play way above average to prove yourself and to keep your job. I also knew that I had a season—two seasons at most—before Coach Gibbs brought in his pick to replace me.

Not only were we having a lousy season, but it was also painfully obvious that the coach and I weren't connecting. If he was hot, I was cold. We weren't *simpatico*, so to speak. During our weekly offensive meetings, I got the feeling that Coach Gibbs wasn't really talking to me. True intentions from both sides of the table were just not being heard or felt.

My job was on the line. So I made a decision. After our fifth loss that season, I drove over to Coach Gibbs's house one late night. I knew it was a risky move. He slept at Redskin Park on Monday, Tuesday, and Wednesday nights, and after the football game on Sunday night, he was the most exhausted man in the world.

I was risking waking up a hibernating bear.

Coach opened the door with a look that was the perfect combination of exhaustion and shock. As he looked at the dark shadow standing before him, I opened with, "Hi, Coach, can we talk?" He let me in, and we sat down on his couch. I didn't give him much time to speculate about why I was there. "Look, Coach, I just don't feel like you and I are on the same page. I feel like we're in meetings together, but we're just . . . there's something missing. There's just something wrong." This was his chance to tell me how he really felt about me. He drew in a long breath and we finally got down to the real issue. "Well, Joe, you have your radio show and you have your TV show, and you have your restaurant. All I want is a quarterback who is totally committed to football and to winning." I straightened up. "Coach, I can be that. I can be the guy that you want me to be. In fact, if you tell me right now, I'll cancel the shows, I'll sell the restaurant, and I'll remove myself from everything, if that's what it takes to prove to you that I want to be your quarterback. But before I do that, I would like you to give me the chance to prove that I can be your quarterback."

That night, we truly became a united front. Starting with the sixth game of the 1981 NFL season, the Redskins became a force to be reckoned with. For the remainder of 1981, we were 8–3. In 1982, we finished the season 8–1 and beat the Dolphins to win Super Bowl XVII. In 1983, we were 14–2 and played the Raiders in Super Bowl XVIII. The following year, we won the Conference championship. Then in 1985, after ten games, my career was over.

Obviously, there were more forces at work than the connection Coach and I made through our heart-to-heart "I can be that guy" conversation. Coach modified the offense and changed the way he used some of the team's talents. Nevertheless, it was also because I decided that my job—my only job—was to be the starting quarterback of the Washington Redskins. Not only that, but I also made it my daily goal to *stay* the starting quarterback of the Washington Redskins. I was highly specific with my goal.

I will ask you again: *What price are you willing to pay to be special?* Here's a story I love that shows the kind of commitment it takes to be a champion and the price it often takes to be special. Ronnie Lott was a renowned defensive back for the San Francisco 49ers for over a decade. He is a four-time Super Bowl champ, a ten-time Pro-Bowler, a Hall of Famer, and among the greatest ever to play the game. At the end of the 1985 season, fullback Timmy Newsome crushed the little finger of Ronnie's left hand. The doctor told Ronnie, "We need to perform a complex bone graft surgery to fix this. But if we do it, you're going to miss the playoffs and probably another shot at the Super Bowl."

 Can you decide right now what price you are willing to pay to achieve your goals?

Ronnie thought for a minute, then asked, "What are my options?"

The doctor said, "Well, we can amputate the upper part of your finger, and you won't miss work."

Without hesitation, Ronnie replied, "Take the finger."

What a legend. I mean, no one is *that* committed, right? After I heard this story, I saw Ronnie at a golf tournament and asked him to let me see his left hand.

I'm here to tell you that the upper part of his left little finger is no longer there.

When I saw it for myself, I asked Ronnie one of my favorite questions. "Why? Why would you do that? You're the best to ever play the position. You're a Hall of Famer. You've got Super Bowl rings. Why?"

His reply has always stayed with me. "Joe, they wanted me to miss a day of work."

The man literally gave up a piece of himself in order to be able to go to work. It's the kind of sacrifice few would ever make. And here's a lesson to be learned from it: When we look at the accomplishments of great entrepreneurs, artists, musicians, and athletes, we see the finished product. But we don't understand the price they paid along the way to get there.

I'm not saying you're going to have to choose between your body parts and success, but you do have to make your mind up that you're going to be special. You have to make your mind up that your goals are going to be SMART and that you are willing to pay your dues to accomplish them. Being more than average and being the kind of person who makes a mark in this world takes real effort, real goal-setting, and a real champion-level commitment—and extreme passion.

Learning from the Pain

After my career-ending injury, I would have given anything to get back in the game—but it wasn't meant to be. People always ask me if Lawrence Taylor ever came to see me while I was in the hospital. He didn't come see me in person, but he did call. It was the Tuesday morning after that fateful night when the nurse walked into the room and said, "Mr. Theismann, Mr. Taylor's on the phone. Would you like to speak to him?"

A wave of emotion washed over me. "Gimme the phone."

She handed me the receiver. "LT, is that you?"

"Yeah, Joe, how ya doing?"

"Not very well, LT."

"Why?"

"*Why?* You broke both of the bones in my leg, for cryin' out loud!"

LT replied, "You gotta understand something, Joe. I don't do anything halfway. Gotta run now. Goodbye."

Kidding or not, you have to admire that kind of "all in" attitude. I have known LT for years, and I think he's the greatest outside linebacker that ever played the game of football. I suppose if you're going to get taken out of the game, then you might as well get taken out by the best of the best.

LT and I have played golf together from time to time, and the only rule I have for our games is this: Lawrence is *not allowed* to stand on my left side. I want to be able to see him at all times.

If I had to do everything over again, there isn't much about my life I would change. However, I still don't want to relive that break. A few years after the injury, Lawrence and I were sitting together at a sports bar in New Jersey. A highlight reel came on the big screen, and that infamous sack that ended my career made the highlights. As they showed the break in slow motion, both of us instantly looked away from the screen.

 In thirty-four years, I've watched the replay of my leg break only once. I don't need to see it. I lived it.

The night after they replayed the injury on TV, I said to Lawrence, "You know, LT, you and I are going to be linked to my injury forever. We all know how it affected me. It ended my career. But I'm curious, how did it affect you?"

He replied, "Joe, I learned a great lesson that night. I learned that no matter how great you are at what you do, it could be over in an instant. So every day, every play, you have to make the best of it. Because if you don't, you may never be given that opportunity again."

That, my friends, is exactly what makes this so much more than a book about some guy who played football. This is a book about *opportunity*, about making every day count. You don't know when the "breaks" are going to come, so you have to live every day like you're living your last, best chance. And the process starts with setting the right goals that articulate the vision you have for your life.

After my injury, I had to reassess my goals. It couldn't be all about me anymore. Sure, there are things that I wanted to accomplish, but being a better person, partner, and friend had to be a part of the new goals I set for myself. I wanted to be a giver rather than a taker.

BONUS #3

A Saint Who Kept His Edge

IN 2009, DURING THE bye week for the New Orleans Saints, the players had the option to take some much-needed time off, so they could relax, unwind, and bond with their families. Everyone expected the players to take advantage of that week off, even if it was just for a few days. Bye weeks are known as the downtime that players *need* in order to shift their focus to their lives outside of the structured, minute-by-minute routine of the NFL season.

That year, Saints quarterback Drew Brees decided to do things a little differently. On the Sunday he had off, Drew went straight to the one place that other players avoid during their bye week: He headed over to the practice facility and went through a simulated game. It was a small sacrifice, and yet no one else was doing it. Drew went above and beyond to keep his competitive edge. He knew he needed to stay sharp.

The Saints made it to Super Bowl XLIV that year and played against Peyton Manning and the Indianapolis Colts, who were favored to win by five. But as the Saints beat the Colts 31–17 and Drew Brees was named MVP, it looked like Drew's small sacrifice had paid off in a big way.

Did that one day really make a difference in the Saints winning? We'll never know for sure. But I guarantee that it didn't hurt.

After their victory, I asked Drew what had set him apart that year, and he said, "It was all about visualization." Drew knew what it took to be special, he visualized it, he made it his goal, and then he achieved it. No one would have thought twice about Drew taking his bye week to rest and unwind. Yet he chose the path less traveled. And it just so happened to be the year that his team won the Super Bowl.

Coincidence? Not likely.

"You have a choice.

You can choose to be *pretty good*,

or you can choose to be *great*."

4

CUSTOMER SERVICE
People Are the Reason We're in Business

That little extra will always get you that little extra.

Pretty Good Is Pretty Bad

Charles Osgood is one of the pioneers of broadcasting. For over forty years, he's been telling America stories on the radio and television, and he's won three Emmys and a few Peabody Awards along the way. What a lot of people don't realize about Charles is that he was actually born Charles Osgood Wood. But after landing his first gig at ABC News in Manhattan, he discovered there was already a newsman named Charles Woods at the network. So he decided to create an *opportunity* to differentiate himself by dropping his surname.

Four years later, in 1971, Charles capitalized on another *opportunity* when he had the chance to fill in as a last-minute weekend anchor replacement. That opportunity turned into a distinguished career with the CBS network that has since spanned four decades. Charles is best known for being the host of *CBS News Sunday Morning*, but he was also the host of *The Osgood File* on

CBS Radio, where he delighted audiences with his insights on everything from major news stories to whimsical human interest pieces. He even performed in rhyme during some of his shows, which is why he is known as the poet-in-residence at CBS News. One of the poems that he read on his program particularly resonated with me.

In his poem "Pretty Good Is Pretty Bad," Charles Osgood references students and teachers, schools and towns, and even a nation as being pretty good. But if you're looking for greatness, you'll find that pretty good won't get you there because that means you're pretty bad as well.

If you settle for being *pretty good* in life, you'll discover that it actually produces a *pretty bad* attitude and, ultimately, *pretty bad* results. To illustrate how *pretty good* isn't anything close to *good*, think about this: How many times a day does somebody ask you, "How are you?"

The question has become so commonplace that the words themselves have lost all meaning. And most of the time, when cashiers, waiters, and even our business colleagues or acquaintances ask, "How are you?" very few of us answer truthfully. Think back on the last time you were asked that question. I bet that if you answered, "Good," it meant your day was going along fine. But if you answered, "Pretty good," I'll wager that response actually meant, "I'm not so good, but you don't really want to know that."

Pretty good really is *pretty bad*. So why strive to be *pretty good* in life? Being *pretty good* in business certainly won't get you far. As customers, when we are treated *pretty good*, we aren't in any hurry to do business with that person or company again. In order to build loyalty—in both business and personal relationships—you have to be willing to do more than just enough. You have to be willing to go further than *pretty good*. If you want to be remembered, and if you want to win, you have to be *great*.

Exceptional Customer Service

We all need a game plan for life and work. We wouldn't even think about playing a football game without a plan in place. When it comes to creating the right blueprint to follow, I've actually never seen a *bad* game plan—just lousy execution. The game plan you create for your life should include the elements we've discussed so far in this book: finding opportunities to create a competitive advantage for yourself and your business, developing a championship attitude, and setting SMART goals.

Next up is what I call achieving *exceptional customer service* (not *pretty good* or *adequate* customer service). At its core, customer service boils down to people–people relationships. A few years ago, I was hired by a guy named Nick Gromicko to shoot some promotional videos for use in the inspection industry. I agreed to five mini-commercials for him, no more. Everything was going well, but we had surpassed the number of videos for which I was contractually obligated. Nick then called for a break and asked me if I had remembered something from the past. He reminded me that after I won a Super Bowl, my team was worried I would injure my throwing hand by continuing to sign autographs. I insisted I wanted to continue signing so they manufactured a bronze stamp of my signature that I could use instead. Well, fast-forward thirty-five years and my client, who had reminded me of this, handed me that very bronze signature stamp. He had taken the time, as well as the effort, to track it down and purchase it from a collector. I was about to remind him that we had exceeded the number of videos I was being paid for when he handed me the stamp. I couldn't believe it. After all these years, he had found it and given it to me. It was a remarkable addition to my collection. Shocked and delighted, I asked him how many more video clips we still needed to shoot. He replied: "I need fourteen more, Joe." My response was: "Well, Nick, we better get started." The point is that money isn't everything. Effort combined with a personal touch will often work even better. It certainly worked on me.

In the world of sports, customer service comprises the way we interact with teammates, coaches, and fans. In the world of business, it's how we interact with our co-workers, employees, customers, and clients—in other words, those we serve, and those who serve us. Exceptional customer service can even include the way we handle our relationships with friends and family members.

When it comes to my own personal customer service motto, there's a little quote by John Maxwell that has sat on top of my desk for years. It goes like this: *"People don't care how much you know, until they know how much you care."*

To me, that is the very *essence* of service. Showing that you care about more than your own interests will instantly add to your credibility and build unparalleled loyalty. People will move heaven and earth to work with other people and companies who have proven that they truly care about their customers, clients, and friends.

But before we can discover how to attain an exceptional level of service, we are going to look at the current standard of service today—that is, *pretty good* service.

Pretty Good Is the Norm

It's rare for our customer service experiences to be anything more than *pretty good*. For example, think about the last time you walked into a bank. Did you notice the vault behind the tellers? Typically, that vault, with its huge wads of money, is sitting wide open. Now, you're just there to cash a check, so you walk over to the table to fill out a deposit slip. And there you discover that a 19¢ pen is chained to the table. The vault's wide open, but the 19¢ pen is chained down—and if you've had the same experience I have, most of the time, that tethered pen doesn't even work. Most banks do this, and we accept it. After all, it's the norm, right? But maybe it's only the norm because we've come to expect *mediocre* as the norm.

In business, it's perfectly fine to want to maximize profit, but there comes a point when you have to ask yourself: At what cost do I want to increase my bottom line? If that increase can only be attained by providing *pretty good* rather than *exceptional* service, then I have a feeling that any increase you see in profits will be short-lived. It also won't do much for your brand or your image. There is simply too much competition out there today—in every industry—not to put the needs of the customer first.

 When you sacrifice service to increase the bottom line, you'll usually end up falling short in both.

Personally, I always make a point of prioritizing the needs of my clients. When I'm preparing to give a presentation, I usually have a conference call with my client to find out exactly what they are looking for. Yes, I *could* just show up, make sure I cover what they are expecting to hear, and be on my way. However, I prefer to do a little bit more. For example, if the client has set up a photo opportunity at an event, instead of taking a few pictures with the attendees and leaving, I let the client know that if they want to send me the photos afterward, I can personalize every picture. I figure I can always be *pretty good*, but I prefer to take the time and effort—even if it's only in a small way—to exceed their expectations.

There are an endless number of ways that small details can make a big difference. A friend of mine named Jimmy was expanding his company by opening up a new location. I called my florist, John, and said, "Hey, John, do me a favor. Send something nice along with a note over to Jimmy congratulating him on the new store, will you?"

John assured me, "Joe, I've been taking care of you for years. Don't even worry about it."

Two days later, I received a call from Jimmy. "Hey, Joe, I love the plant . . . but I really don't understand the card."

"What do you mean?" I asked my friend.

He replied, "The card says, 'Rest in peace.'"

Realizing the mix-up, I said, "Well, Jimmy, my concern is not for you. It's for the other guy who got the card that says, 'Congratulations on your new location.'"

It's the little things that make all the difference when it comes to the level of service you give and receive. Don't make the mistake of assuming that the people you do business with aren't going to look for a better deal, a better relationship, or a better opportunity when your service comes up a little short or is merely satisfactory. *Satisfactory* service is simply not a sustainable model of success.

> Mom-ism: "Joey, a gentleman opens the car door for a lady; a gentleman helps a lady with her coat; a gentleman rises from the dinner table when a lady gets up. These are little things that a gentleman does to let a lady know that she's special and extraordinary."

All these years later, her words echo in my ears. I spend a great deal of time traveling all over the country—and all over the world—and it's fair to say that I've observed a *lot* of people. Whenever I look around at the *pretty good* state of service and at the way we treat each other, I find myself constantly asking this question: *When did chivalry die?*

When did we stop doing little things for people to let them know they're special? When did we grow so complacent in our relationships that we no longer feel the need to show people how much they mean to us? It takes less time than you think to show others how much you care. Cook a special dinner for your partner. Send flowers or a card to someone, even when the occasion doesn't call for it. It's those little things we do that make a world of difference.

The world seems to think that chivalry is dead. But just because something is "the norm" doesn't mean we have to do it that way. There's no such thing as *normal*, anyway. There's no such thing as a *normal* family or *normal* business hours. It's all subjective, right?

That's great news for you because it means that you can create your own norms. It means that you can establish a level of customer service, both in life and in business, based on your *own* standards, not society's. It's okay to do things differently from the way other people do them. In fact, blazing your own extraordinary path can give you the competitive edge you need to win.

Do What Others Won't

What does *great* customer service look like? Like most of us, I've experienced truly great moments of service a few times in my life. One of those moments happened on my way to play golf at Firestone Country Club in Ohio. Firestone Country Club is truly one of the most spectacular golf courses in America. It would be an understatement to say that I was eager to play there. But when I arrived in Cleveland, I discovered that my golf clubs had not made the journey with me and it would take me an hour to get to Firestone. I went to baggage claim and explained my quandary to the young woman behind the counter. I had a tee time already set, and I needed my clubs by that afternoon.

If you've ever dealt with baggage claim, you know that those poor people get yelled at all the time. And as a result, many of them have developed an understandably less-than-stellar opinion of the general public. After I explained my situation to the young woman behind the counter, I braced myself for her response. But what she did next truly surprised me. Instead of saying, "Fill out this form. Here's the number to call. We'll deliver it to you when we can," she picked up the phone, called the baggage claim at Dulles Airport—where I had departed from—and got the head of the baggage claim department on the line.

"I have a gentleman here who needs his golf clubs," she said. "They were not on the plane with him. What is the status?"

When the manager reported that my clubs were still there at Dulles, she responded, "Well, I'd like to talk to the person who is going to put those clubs on a plane."

I would have loved to see the look on the manager's face at that moment. He paused on the other end of the line before replying, "Um, I'll get back to you."

But she was unyielding. "No, I will stay on the line until you tell me that those clubs are on a plane headed this way."

I am happy to report that my clubs arrived in time for me to make my tee time, entirely due to the efforts of that young lady. Wherever she is today, I'd like to say to her, "You are an exceptional person, and United Airlines is lucky to have you. Thank you so much for going the extra mile to help me, when you could have just as easily done less." It took her five minutes to handle the situation, and yet those five minutes will stay with me for years to come.

Here's another example of a minor yet hugely impactful gesture. My insurance agent is named Al Opas. I bought my first policy from Al when I was twenty-one years old. It's been a number of decades since Al and I have actually spoken, but every year on my birthday, I receive a card from him. I have many other insurance agents, but none of them has ever taken the time to wish me a happy birthday with a card—and that's precisely why I can recall Al's name. Al distinguished himself through a little bit of extra effort.

You have to be willing to do what others won't do. Notice that I didn't say what others *can't* do—because we *all* have the capacity to show kindness and take small extra steps. The problem is that most people simply are not willing to.

Let me share a few more examples of outstanding customer service. I was staying at the Westin Hotel in Atlanta, and one evening, I walked into one of their restaurants wearing black pants. I hadn't noticed that there were white napkins on the table, but someone else did; just as I was being seated, a waiter walked up to me and said, "Excuse me, sir, I'll be right back." He grabbed the white napkin off the table. Before I knew it, he'd replaced it with a black one. He'd noticed my black pants, and he didn't want any white lint rubbing off on them. Those are the kinds of details that make lasting impressions.

Here's one more. Have you ever walked into Home Depot without knowing where to find a certain item? That store is so vast; sometimes it's hard not to get lost. Well, if you ask one of the employees where to find a product, they don't just *tell* you. They *show* you. They stop whatever they are doing and walk you right up to the product in question.

Little Things

Why do I remember all of these little things? It's because "little things" *do* make a difference. Customer service is *all* about the little things.

Part of doing what others don't do involves embarking upon an endless quest for knowledge. When it comes to running a business, there is never a time when it's okay to stop learning about your customers, your product line, or your industry. *When you stop learning, you stop living.*

Let's say you work at a bar, and a customer requests a drink with a specific brand of vodka. *Pretty good* bartenders would say, "We don't have that brand," and then wait in silence while the patron decides on an alternative.

On the other hand, an *exceptional* bartender would say, "Unfortunately, we don't carry that brand of vodka, but we have something similar. Here, let me give you a sample so that you can taste it for yourself." Was that hard to do? Not at all—it simply required some product and brand knowledge. Will that bartender get a nice tip? I bet so! And it will all be thanks to product knowledge, which enables you to answer people's questions and discover the best solutions for them.

 It takes less energy than you think: The smallest efforts can actually make the biggest difference.

To elevate your service from *pretty good* to *extraordinary,* all you have to do is decide to start taking small extra steps. It will take less energy than you think. Something as simple as recognizing repeat customers and remembering clients' names will help you stand out from the crowd. Whatever you choose to do to create a competitive edge, it all comes down to asking yourself this question: *"What small steps can I take to show my customers, clients, friends, and family that I truly care about them?"*

Notre Dame's Indelible Impact

I was blessed to have the opportunity to play football at one of the greatest universities on earth. The University of Notre Dame wasn't just where I obtained my degree and launched my professional football career. Notre Dame also played an instrumental role in shaping my views on people–people relationships.

What many people don't realize is that my journey to become a Fighting Irishman was a unique one. When I was deciding which university to attend, I considered many options. After much deliberation, I narrowed my choices down to five universities—North Carolina State, Wake Forest, The University of North Carolina, Penn State, and the University of Notre Dame. My head football coach in high school, Ron Wojcicki, had deep connections with North Carolina State, having gone to school there and playing behind quarterback Roman Gabriel—who went on to become an NFL legend.

For some reason, I thought that my coach's experience was the perfect reason why *I* should also go to North Carolina State University. My choice had nothing to do with academics. In fact, it had nothing to do with anything other than the fact that my football coach, whom I admired greatly, had gone there and had a great experience.

After I decided to attend NC State, all the recruiting came to a halt, and the smoke cleared. It was then that something told me to do a little more searching. I decided to take a trip to Notre Dame, even though I had already signed with NC State.

From the moment I stepped onto the Notre Dame campus, I knew I was in a special place. It's impossible to walk onto the campus and not be blown away by its beauty and grandeur. The campus looks like it was taken straight out of mid-century Italy or France. It has a majestic, otherworldly feel to it in so many ways, and I could just *feel* its rich history.

The campus was massive, with 143 buildings (these days it's more like 200 buildings) located on two quads. The Main Quad is filled with trees. In the fall, it looks like an endless sea of yellows and reds as the leaves change color and cover the ground. The University's Historic Center—made up of the Basilica, the Golden Dome, and Washington Hall—was built in the early decades of the University in the 1870s. The magnificent Theodore Hesburgh Library, with its gorgeous reflecting pool and impressive façade, is extraordinary by anyone's standards.

Needless to say, my first impression was a good one. Then it got even better. My hosts during my tour of the campus and athletic facilities were Rocky Bleier, who would go on to be a four-time World Champion with the Pittsburgh Steelers and a Vietnam vet, and Dan Harshman, another running back. I was then invited to play basketball at the Rockne Memorial, the only basketball court on campus at the time. The coaches liked to assess players' overall athletic abilities by watching them play a game of hoops.

It was truly a magical weekend. After my tour ended, I boarded a plane for home with no doubt in my mind. I knew what I had to do. We landed in Newark, New Jersey, and as I walked off the plane, my dad approached me with, "So, what did you think?"

"Dad, I have to go to Notre Dame."

When my father asked me—and when people ask me, even today—why I chose the University of Notre Dame, my response simply was and is, "It just felt right."

It's amazing to me how many times in life we choose to go against our gut instincts, even though, in most cases, we'd be better off trusting those feelings. Instead, we sit down, analyze, focus on the minutiae, and we ultimately end up making a decision for the reasons that look right on paper. And yet later, looking back, we realize that our gut instincts probably would have yielded far better results. As they say, hindsight is 20/20.

Ultimately, I went where my heart led me. And my decision to attend the University of Notre Dame is one of those times when I'm glad I went with my gut. In retrospect, I realize now that my gut reaction was based on two things. First, it was based on my overall first impressions of the campus. It was pristine. It was impressive. You could feel the rich history and the pride that the students and faculty had in their school. Second, everyone on campus made me feel special at every point during my visit. They even asked two of their players to drop everything in order to walk around with a skinny kid from Jersey. It made me feel like I was being inducted into an exclusive and privileged club—and I truly was.

You can strive to make every customer, friend, and loved one feel that kind of special status when they interact with you by making a few changes to the way you interact with them. It really is about the details: Remember people's names. Recognize others for a job well done. Give them a pat on the back. Help someone carry a heavy load to his or her car. These are just a few of the countless little gestures that can make someone's day—or even make an indelible impact on their lives.

The Foundation of Customer Service

During my time at Notre Dame, I had many significant experiences that shaped much of what was to come in my life. My career in public speaking and my recognition of the importance of customer service began at Notre Dame as well, right in the classroom. There were two courses in particular during my time at the university that have served me in life more than any others: *Speech* and *Argumentation.* In those classes, I discovered that when it comes to people–people relationships—whether you are connecting one-on-one or speaking to a room of thousands—proper communication skills are at the root of everything.

As a quarterback at Notre Dame, I was occasionally asked to speak at functions, like communion breakfast. Those were my first experiences with public speaking. And as fate would have it, I had quite a few more chances to speak after winning the World Championship in 1983. As I began to deliver speeches more frequently, I recognized—from the instruction I'd received at Notre Dame—how to communicate my thoughts and ideas in a way that resonated with people and got them truly excited about something.

Because of that strong foundation in communication, I was able to do something that few former-players-turned-commentators do. Soon after playing in Super Bowl XVII and Super Bowl XVIII, I was given the chance to broadcast Super Bowl XIX with Frank Gifford and Don Meredith. O. J. Simpson was scheduled to be in the booth with them, but ABC decided to replace him with me for the matchup between the San Francisco 49ers and the Miami Dolphins in Palo Alto, California. The biggest game in sports became my first true entry into broadcasting.

Overnight, I had gone from NFL quarterback to prime-time commentator. After that, I started getting invited to a lot of corporate functions in a variety of industries, ranging from healthcare to finance to manufacturing. I spoke at annual company retreats, Chamber of Commerce luncheons, and everything in between. That was the point in my career when I started to notice how people focus on the same things in the business world that we focused on in football: goals, attitudes, competition, service, teamwork, and motivation. When you think about it, those are the same areas that we must emphasize in our personal lives, as well.

I took what I learned at Notre Dame and in the world of football, and I created a presentation that I believe is equally relevant to the world of sports, the world of business, and our own personal lives. For the past thirty-plus years, I have been honored to have the opportunity to share with people how each of those areas parallel one another. I've given my presentation over 1,800 times to almost a million people. Through a lot of trial and error—and with the wisdom received from my parents, coaches, respected businesspeople, teammates, and other special people—I am able to share a game plan for success that I believe can empower people to find the success they want to achieve in their own lives.

Those two classes at Notre Dame were invaluable sources of training in my life. That is why I recommend that every student invest in some type of a speech course. Sooner or later, you are going to need it, whether you use what you learn to ace an interview or to craft a compelling email to your best client.

Sure, you can send a text, you can post something on Instagram, and you can connect on LinkedIn—those are all great. But at some point in your career, you're going to have to sit down with someone face-to-face and explain why *you* are the best person for the job. Having the skills to be able to communicate your intentions is vitally important. And that is why proper communication skills are at the heart of my customer service message.

Trust Your Gut

I had the incredible opportunity to play in two Super Bowls, but I am not in the exclusive club of quarterbacks who have the honor of winning the big trophy more than once. Speaking of that ill-fated Super Bowl XVIII, many of you might remember the interception that I threw just before halftime (if you don't, that's fine with me—I've tried to forget it myself). Well, like everything else in my life, there's a story behind it.

We had twelve seconds to go in the half, and we had the ball on our own twelve-yard line. During a timeout, I went to the sidelines and asked Coach Gibbs what play he wanted me to run.

"Run Rocket Screen," came Coach's reply.

Rocket Screen was a play that had served us well that season, and it had actually gone for ninety yards against the Raiders when we played them earlier in the year. Despite this fact, I told Coach that I didn't feel good about putting the ball into the air with as little time as we had on the clock—not to mention how backed up we were. Still, we *were* 14 and 2 for the season, plus two victories in the playoffs, and Coach had done such a great job all year. Why was I arguing with those kinds of results?

Remember what I said about trusting your gut? Well, in that moment, something just didn't feel right. As I turned away from Coach Gibbs to go back onto the field, I glanced back, thinking he might change his mind and call a different play.

Instead, he pointed his finger at me and said in the most emphatic way, "Run it."

I did what I had to do. I called the play, went to the line of scrimmage, took the snap, and for a moment, it looked like the play might work. Except for one problem. A linebacker by the name of Jack Squirek was in man-to-man coverage on my halfback, Joe Washington. Yet we were expecting a zone coverage. We were expecting that each defensive player would be given a zone to cover, rather than having each member of the defense guarding a corresponding player on our team.

As I turned to let the ball go, I noticed Jack Squirek breaking toward Joe. I knew there were going to be some unpleasant consequences—and boy, was I right. Squirek caught the ball, pranced into the end zone, and we went into halftime trailing the Raiders 21–3.

For years, I took the blame for that lousy play in Super Bowl XVIII. Finally, at a fundraiser five years later, I had the chance to bring up my misgivings about that play to Coach Gibbs. I said to him, "Coach, that call you made in Super Bowl XVIII before the half was one of the worst I'd ever seen."

Coach didn't miss a beat. "It may have been, but I have to tell you, Joe. That pass was one of the worst I'd ever seen."

You see, folks, success is *not* guaranteed. And just because you've tasted it once, don't think for a minute that it will stick around—especially if you lose the burning desire that it takes to *stay* successful. Success in business will only come (and remain) for those who treat every person, customer, and friend like they themselves want to be treated. This is why it's a good idea to make the good ol' Golden Rule an integral part of your customer service strategy. In fact, that is exactly what the most successful people and businesses do.

Customer Service Starts at Home

So often, we think of *customer service* or *client service* as performing a duty for or providing assistance to someone who will buy something from us in return. In reality, customer service also exists *inside* every company. It comes down to how we treat one another inside our organizations. Having the right attitude about service requires you to shift your thinking about the concept. You need to realize that customer service is not just for those whom you want to sell something to. On the contrary, customer service starts at home.

We've talked a lot about my customer service experiences in the business world, at the University of Notre Dame, and on the field. However, my understanding of what it takes to be *exceptional* at service started at my home in South River, New Jersey, many years ago.

With a combined income of $12,000, my parents certainly weren't wealthy by anyone's standards. But when I was growing up, I didn't know that. I felt I had a blessed life because I owned a baseball. When its cover came off, we wrapped it in electrical tape, and I had another baseball. I also owned a bat. When the bat broke, we put a nail in it, wrapped some tape around the break, and my bat was as good as new. I also owned a football. When the laces broke on my football, we tied it back together with a shoe-string, and my football was shipshape once again. Maybe my things weren't as fancy as the other kids' stuff, but my parents gave me whatever I needed. And most importantly, I felt loved.

I quite often mention my mother's great influence in my life through her *Mom-isms*. But my father was also incredible in his own unique way. He shaped the way I treat everyone, from close friends to business associates to the most casual acquaintances.

My father left school to support our family, and he also served our country in the United States Army. For those reasons and so much more, my dad is truly my hero. Heroes are the people who sacrifice great things so that we can have a better life. Heroes are people like our young men and women in the military, police, firefighters, and all the others who are out there protecting us and standing up for us on a daily basis.

My hero and father, Joseph John Theismann, worked at a gas station that he owned for twenty-five years. After he sold the station, he worked thirteen hours a day, six days a week in my uncle's liquor store for another twenty-five years. He had an hour for dinner, so he'd drive fifteen minutes from the liquor store to get home, take thirty minutes for dinner, and then promptly leave to drive the fifteen minutes back to the store. Six out of seven days a week, I saw my dad for half an hour before ten o'clock at night.

Then came Sundays. On Sunday mornings, we went to church. After coming home from church, we'd have our one big family meal of the week. After the meal, my dad would plop down in his easy chair, close his eyes, and be sound asleep in a heartbeat. Within ten minutes, little Joey would come running up, shake his arm, and say, "Dad, Dad, come on, let's go play football," or "Come on, let's go outside and play baseball." Without hesitation, my dad would get up from his chair and go outside to throw the ball around with his son.

Within a few minutes of us being outside, my buddies would run by, headed for the school. Our house was two blocks away from the high school, grammar school, and lots of athletic fields, so my friends were always stopping by to ask me to join them on their way to play. They'd say, "Hey, Joey, come on, let's go."

Every time, I'd run after them as I yelled over my shoulder, "Bye, Dad, see ya later."

With that, he'd go back into the house, and I'd go off and play ball.

Year after year after year, this was our Sunday routine. Yet, never once, as he sat resting in that chair—after putting in an eighty-hour workweek—did my father turn to me and say, "Joey, look, I know you and your buddies are going to be taking off in ten minutes. I'm really tired. How about if you give me a chance to catch some rest?" My dad never, ever said *no* to a chance to spend a few minutes with me, even though he knew exactly how it was going to play out.

I've mentioned that both of my parents are gone, but their lessons will live on with me forever. My dad taught me that small sacrifices make the biggest difference. He showed me that you can make a powerful impact in a person's life—whether it is a customer, a co-worker, a friend, or a family member—simply by saying "yes" when it'd be simpler to say "no." It would have been so easy for him to say, "Not today, Joey." *But he never did.* That small, seemingly insignificant decision is one of the things that elevated my father to hero status in my eyes. My dad was a truly special man, and I can only hope to be half the man he was.

Champions Don't Do "Pretty Good"

If you think about your life up to this point, I bet you can only name a small handful of people who have powerfully impacted your life in a lasting way. If you can name even one, consider yourself blessed. But even if you have none, you can still aspire to become that kind of influence in someone else's life.

Aside from my parents, I've been lucky to know a few other truly special people in my lifetime. One of those individuals is Peyton Manning—you've probably heard of him. Peyton is a five-time MVP, a two-time World Champion quarterback, and he holds so many records that it would be exhausting to try to list all of them.

Those achievements make him a very special guy, but here's a little something that I think makes him even more spectacular. When I was broadcasting at ESPN, I had the opportunity to be a part of numerous interviews with Peyton. Before a show would air, we'd all sit down in a pre-show production meeting. There were around seven people in the room, along with Peyton. And he called every last person, no matter who it was, by his or her first name. If Jay Rothman, our producer, asked him a question, Peyton would start with, "Now, Jay, this is what we would do in that situation . . ." If Suzy Kolber asked him something, he'd say, "Suzy, that's really a good question . . ."

I was so impressed by that small detail of remembering and using each and every person's name. It demonstrated the fact that he had taken the time to get to know everyone on a first-name basis. Now, knowing this, should we be surprised at how meticulous and decisive he was on the field? I, for one, am not at all surprised. So many little things Peyton does off the field separate him from the crowd.

Be the kind of person who makes others feel welcome and important.

I've said it before, and I'll say it again: It's the little things that create the difference between *good* and *great*. For that reason, I have taken the lessons I've learned from people like Peyton Manning and applied them to my own business ventures, including my restaurant in Alexandria, Virginia. At the restaurant, we've impressed upon the staff the importance of making everyone who walks through the door feel comfortable by welcoming them and thanking them for choosing to dine with us. Personal touches like that go a long way toward building trust and fostering a sense of loyalty.

Making people feel welcome is a seemingly minor, but often overlooked, element of service. I can't tell you how many times I've walked into a gym, restaurant, or business and observed two employees in conversation, completely unaware of my presence. Sometimes, it can take several minutes for them to even notice me or ask what I need. All the while, I stand there wondering, *Am I invisible, or do they just not care?*

When you walk into Joe Theismann's Restaurant, we want you to be acknowledged. We want you to be seated quickly. We want you to see smiles and friendly faces. If your job requires you to interact with other people, customers, or clients, make it your goal to help them feel comfortable. Make it your goal to make them glad that they are taking some of their valuable time to speak with you, frequent your establishment, or listen to what you have to say.

Thanking Those Along the Way

As an added touch in my business interactions, I also handwrite my "thank-you" letters. Now, I don't profess to be a grammarian. What you get from me certainly isn't going to be perfect—but neither am I. However, I do believe that taking the time to sit down and write a letter is important.

I learned this from an experience I had a number of years ago. After I gave a presentation to a large company, I received a beautifully worded, typed letter from the CEO. Here's the thing—it wasn't signed. It had clearly been dictated, but he hadn't taken the five seconds needed to sign the letter. When I saw that, I thought, *Does this guy really care? Did he even hear what I said? Or is he just going through the motions and doing what the rules of etiquette demand?*

Going through the motions is not for people who want to make a difference and be truly great at what they do. Some of you may be thinking, *Joe, I have a lot of correspondence to reply to, and I can't handwrite every letter. I can't stop and reach out to every customer, every client, or every acquaintance. Come on. Nobody has time to do that.*

I understand that it's difficult to handwrite every letter. But there are lots of ways to add a personal touch, and it takes less time than you think. For example, at the base of a dictated note or thank-you letter, you could take fifteen seconds to write something in your own script—one or two sentences relating a special, unique detail that stood out to you about your experience with that person.

I promise you that the next time you get a letter or a note with something handwritten at the bottom, that handwritten section is what you will read first, no matter how elegant the stationery or how well phrased the sentiments.

If you can't or won't take a few moments to connect with your clients and customers in a meaningful way, why are you in business? If your answer is "for the bottom line," then I have a little secret to share with you—the most successful, wealthy men and women I know got that way because they consistently made time for others, great and small. They showed people that they cared, which in turn made people care about what they had to say and made them *want* to do business with them.

There's a saying that I like to use to close my presentations: "It's nice to be important, but it's a lot more important to be nice." Yes, being important is nice, but I also believe that *everyone* is important, and making others feel important is why we're here. That is the heart of customer service.

Businesses and lives don't thrive when all we do is go through the motions. Our lives are not designed to exist on autopilot. You can choose to coast along on autopilot and do "pretty good" in life and business. But is that really what you want? Do you want to be *pretty good* . . . or do you want to be *great*?

The choice is up to you. I encourage you to choose to do the little things that will take you from providing *pretty good* service to delivering *exceptional* service. Always strive to exceed someone's expectations.

BONUS #4
Time Spent = Value Received

WHEN I FIRST JOINED the Redskins in 1974, there were no posters of me for sale. There were also no footballs with my name on them at the stadium gift shop. But I didn't let any of that stop me from deciding to make my own posters and sell my own footballs.

Some might consider me a raving egomaniac for coming up with such an idea. But really, I was an entrepreneur. I spent $3,000 on printing posters and buying footballs to sign. Then I drove around on my days off to convenience stores, drugstores, and any other place that sold memorabilia, and I tried to sell my products.

In my mind, it was a sound business idea. But here's how it actually turned out: Not counting the considerations of "time value of money" and the gas I used up driving to Timbuktu and back, I invested $3,000; in return, the six-month experience earned me a grand total of $600.

How many minutes do we invest over the course of our life-times in activities that don't yield proportionate results? When it comes to the activities you choose to engage in, that trade-off is something you must consider.

On August 2, 2003, I was broadcasting a game in Tokyo for ESPN—it was the Tampa Bay Buccaneers versus the New York Jets. Before the game, as I was standing on the sidelines with Bucca-neers head coach John Gruden (now the head coach of the Las Vegas Raiders), who delivered an amazing insight to me. He told me to look at the Jets quarterbacks and notice that none of them were wearing wristbands with their plays on them.

Then he asked me to look at the wristbands that his Buccaneers quarterbacks wore, which had every play written down on them. Jon said, "Now, what that means is, the Jets are gonna sit in meet-ings with their QBs during the preseason and memorize all of those plays—and oh, by the way, at least a couple of those guys will probably be cut from the team before the season even starts. As for those who stay, they'll have to spend time coming up with signals to get the plays in. That takes a lot of time and effort. But with my guys, I can hold up one finger on the sideline, they can look down at the play sheet, and call the play. It's as easy as that."

Wow. Now that's "time well spent with value received." Jon didn't waste anyone's time or talents. He found a way to maximize the num-ber of useful hours in the day and even avoided wasting the time of players who weren't ultimately going to be on the team. (And this is from a guy who starts his day at 3:30 a.m.)

Sometimes, you don't know exactly how much a particular time investment will yield until it's already been invested. But when pos-sible, slow down and think about the time your activities require. Ask yourself, "Will the time it takes to do this yield proportionate results?" If the answer is, "probably not," then it's time to move on to the next big idea and leave the time-wasting for somebody else.

Why?

Because champions make the most of every minute they are given.

"Empower people! Ask them to step
outside their personal silos and give
them the opportunity to change the world.
Human capital is not the first line of
defense, but the first line of *offense*."

5

TEAMWORK
Champions Don't Achieve Greatness Alone

The most important position on
your team is every last one of them.

The Power of the Multiplier Effect

The words *team* and *teamwork* are so overused in athletics and in
the world of business that the terms have lost their authenticity.
Therefore, it's useful to remind ourselves what these words really
mean. Being a contributing participant on a team carries with it
the expectation of putting forth one's best effort. It also requires
trusting that your team members will do the same.

When was the last time you thought about what kind of team
member you are, or reflected on how other team members can
meet your needs?

Are *you* a good teammate? What does being a *valued* teammate
really involve? In my years of studying winning sports teams, business teams, and their leaders, these questions have been some of
the driving forces behind my research.

In one way or another, I've been part of a team for nearly all of my life. When I was six years old, I started playing baseball, football, and basketball. At twelve, I joined Pop Warner football. It was also at that age that my love for the game was fully realized. Since then, whether it's at work, at home, or as part of an athletic group, I've been part of a team.

The way I thought about teams changed when I was a member of a team that won a World Championship. I began to discover not just the "secret ingredients" that make a winning team but also the *recipe*. Since then, I've invested tremendous amounts of effort in an attempt to better understand what *teamwork* truly signifies.

In my search for what it means to contribute to something greater than our own selves, I remembered a concept from one of my college economics classes called the multiplier effect:

> The multiplier effect is the effect of a relatively minor factor in precipitating a great change. In economics, it signifies the power of a minor change in one economic factor (such as rate of saving or level of consumer credit) in causing a disproportionate increase or decrease in another (such as gross national product).

The notion behind the *multiplier effect* is precisely what makes teams so powerful. Let's extend the term outside its traditional meaning. When applied to life and business, the definition becomes:

> The multiplier effect is the effect of a single team member in precipitating great change. It signifies the influence that one human being can have when his or her attitude and abilities are combined with the attitudes and abilities of others.

In other words, an individual person can accomplish goals in small increments, but together, a team can accomplish so much more. The multiplier effect bridges the ordinary to the extraordinary. It's what gives teams their incredible strength.

Teams experience the multiplier effect because of the combined "capital" of their members. In fact, there are distinct kinds of capital ("secret ingredients") that come together to make great teams. I learned this from my good friend Fred Paglia, a former North American president of Kraft Foodservice. Fred believes there are three required components of successful teams and companies.

1. Financial Capital—You must have the resources to run your business.
2. Intellectual Capital—You need smart people. If you don't have enough, hire more.
3. Cultural Capital—You must create an environment where people can be their best. Of the three components, this is the most important.

Together, these three critical components embody the idea behind the acronym TEAM: *Together Everyone Achieves More.*

Fred also believes that teams who work to create an "environment of subservience to a purpose" are powerful. "What I have found," Fred says, "is high-performing teams and successful leaders create a subservience to a purpose, and as the team rallies around a purpose, the multiplier effect increases." Marines are a perfect example of this. As a Marine, it's all about the man or woman next to you, not about what you can gain for yourself.

Regardless of the name you give it—TEAM, the multiplier effect, or the combining of capital—the point is that individuals achieve more and reach untold heights when they come together and function as a single, dynamic unit.

Iron Sharpens Iron

In the Bible, Proverbs 27:17 says that, "As iron sharpens iron, so one man sharpens another." This verse illustrates the mutual benefit of rubbing two iron blades together; by doing so, each blade becomes sharper, making both knives more effective.

Likewise, when we are involved in one another's lives, it results in mutual improvement. We *all* need to sharpen and hone our abilities in some way, shape, or form, and being a part of a team allows us to receive the necessary coaching to do so. One person's efforts and skills sharpen those of another.

Teams do more for us than we could ever do for ourselves— and I'm not just talking about their ability to help us win awards or accomplish great things. Awards and trophies are terrific. But if you don't have a friend, loved one, coach, or team member to share your successes and failures with—and if you don't have other people to help you recognize what you've done right, and help you discover where you need to improve—you will never be the kind of champion you *could* be.

Life works better when we are joined together through partnerships and teamwork. Mankind was not made to be alone, nor to work alone. Teams work well because each individual on a team is committed to a common goal and to improving his or her teammate by extension.

Teams are groups of people who are talented in distinct ways.

On their own, people are good—sometimes even really good.

But when people come together, they have a chance to become great.

Many people believe (and I'm one of them) that Jerry Rice is the greatest receiver who ever played football. *But he was only one part of a whole team.* He wouldn't have seen all that success without his teammates. I also believe that Derek Jeter is the greatest shortstop who ever played baseball. *But he, too, was only one part of a team.*

You don't achieve a championship level of success without having the right people on your team—whether it's in government, business, sports, or life. You have to rely on a team to maximize your own talents. You have to join your talents with the talents of others. You have to allow iron to sharpen iron.

Champions don't settle for mediocrity. They don't want to be average. If iron sharpens iron, the opposite is also true: Mediocrity breeds mediocrity. Always remember that a chain is only as strong as its weakest link. It's important that you talk about being the best, and then surround yourself with people who have similar expectations.

A Tree Is Only as Strong as Its Roots

Anyone who wants to achieve great things in life *must* learn how to work together as part of a team. And there is more to being a team than simply coming together. In order to maximize the time and talents of everyone involved, you have to take it a step further. You need to discover what kind of team member you are, what changes you may need to make to become the best team member you can be, and you need to learn what to expect from your teammates. To accomplish this, let's discuss the building blocks of championship teams and winning team environments.

The greatest teams are those that figure out how to incorporate the financial, intellectual, and cultural capital of successful teams and companies into their own planning and actions. And at the heart of that success are the team members themselves.

Four-star general Colin Powell is one of the United States' greatest modern leaders. He has held numerous top positions in our military and government and is one of the most respected authorities on the subject of leadership. In "A Leadership Primer," his presentation on leadership and victory in business and life, General Powell provides lessons for being the best leaders and team members, providing an excellent description of what every leader should look for in a team member in order to give the team the greatest chance for success:

POWELL'S RULE FOR PICKING PEOPLE

Look for intelligence and judgment, and most critically, a capacity to anticipate, to see around corners. Also look for loyalty, integrity, a high energy drive, a balanced ego, and the drive to get things done. How often do our recruitment and hiring processes tap into these attributes? More often than not, we ignore them in favor of length of resumé, degrees, and prior titles. A string of job descriptions a recruit held yesterday seem to be more important than who one is today, what they can contribute tomorrow, or how well their values mesh with those of the organization. You can train a bright, willing novice in the fundamentals of your business fairly readily, but it's a lot harder to train someone to have integrity, judgment, energy, balance, and the drive to get things done. Good leaders stack the deck in their favor right in the recruitment phase.

General Powell's advice cuts through the bureaucracy of typical hiring practices and gets right down to what makes championship teams. The qualities he mentions are the most sought-after traits in people across industries and on any field—whether it is a battlefield, the field of business, or an athletic field. As we discuss the foundations of championship teams, we will expand upon the qualities that General Powell highlights.

I talk about my former Redskins coach Joe Gibbs a lot, and for good reason. He's one of the most insightful and influential people in my life. He is also a man who knows a thing or two about how to put together a winning team. Joe Gibbs can turn almost any group of guys into champions. He is the only NFL coach to ever win three Super Bowls with three different quarterbacks. He also won multiple championships with his NASCAR racing team (a championship that is now known as the Monster Energy NASCAR Cup Series). He has the ability to convert what he has to work with into something great. And he does so using simple, but powerful, team-building strategies.

Joe Gibbs is a man who knows the "secret recipe for success." As it turns out, it isn't really much of a secret. You have to have a plan. You have to be able to communicate that plan. You need to find the right people to fit into that plan. And you have to empower those people to do their job. You may have figured this out already, but there are no shortcuts in life. Real, sustainable success takes hard work, dedication, and the right people

Back in 1991, when Coach Gibbs was preparing for his fourth Super Bowl appearance, I asked him the question that I've asked several successful leaders: *"What do you look for in a championship individual?"*

I didn't ask him what he looked for in a player, because *anyone* can play the game. As Urban Meyer says, "It's so easy to be average. It takes a little something to be special. Why be average?" I wasn't looking for what it took to "make the team" or what it took to be listed on the roster. I wanted to know what, in Coach's eyes, created champions.

He replied, "Joe, I look for three things: character, intelligence, and ability."

I responded, "Sure, Coach, but everybody's looking for those three things."

He looked at me in that way only he could and said, "No, Joe, that's the *order* in which I look for qualities in people."

Many people might assume that a World Champion head coach looks for ability first. Not Coach Gibbs. His eyes are always focused first on character, then on intelligence, and finally on ability. His answer made me think about what really is most important in others.

What exists under the surface of what we can see that allows championship teams to soar to new heights?

Coach's words made me realize that, like a mighty tree, the groundwork of a championship team must be strong and firmly embedded through four fundamental roots.

Root #1: Character

Coach Gibbs listed *character* first. There's a saying I love with regard to character from famed politician and editor Horace Greeley: "Fame is a vapor; popularity an accident; riches take wings, the only earthly certainty is oblivion; no man can foresee what a day may bring forth."

Joe told me that every last one of us is going to experience tough times in our lives. The question isn't *if* you'll have to ride some stormy seas, but how you will choose to navigate them. What is your reaction to the uncomfortable and painful parts of life? Those reactions reveal your character and say a lot about what kind of teammate or friend you will be.

Lucian Truscott, a World War II general and later deputy director of the CIA, once shared his thoughts on character: "Character is who you are, reputation is who people think you are." With that in mind, what does your character reveal about you? Only you can answer that question. And to do so, you must examine how you approach the trials of life. I highly recommend taking the time to think about what your character says about you and the kind of team member you are to others. No matter how you look at it, the character of each team member is the foundation upon which great teams are built.

Root #2: Intelligence

Next, Coach Gibbs listed *intelligence.* Functioning with a high level of intelligence has grown more and more important in our current culture. Staying ahead of the competition requires increasingly complex strategies, thorough planning, and lightning-fast, accurate execution. I've been in the presence of millionaires and billionaires, but money has never impressed me. On the other hand, people who have extensive knowledge about something? Now *that's* impressive.

Knowledge is power, whether it's street smarts or book smarts. You don't need to have a 4.0 GPA or be a member of Mensa International to be smart. However, you *do* need to stay sharp, pay attention, study your competition, be coachable, and strive to better yourself at every single opportunity.

Root #3: Work Ethic

Before we get to Coach Gibbs's third and final criterion, I want to share some insights from another leader. I once had the opportunity to visit with a coach named Al Saunders. In a career spanning over three decades in pro football, Coach Saunders has been a head coach of the San Diego Chargers and an offensive coordinator for the Kansas City Chiefs, Washington Redskins, St. Louis Rams, and Oakland Raiders. During our visit, I asked Al the same question I asked Coach Gibbs: "What do you look for in a championship individual?"

His answer surprised me. "I want to make sure they are members of the 'able' family: reliable, accountable, and available."

Coach Saunders didn't list talent; he didn't even list intelligence or ability. He wanted the right work ethic in his players. When you boil it down, being reliable, accountable, and available all revolve around how hard you are willing to work to achieve success.

 Your work ethic reveals more about you than words.

Being *reliable* means that if you are asked to do a job, you do that job to the best of your ability. It means that your team can count on you to get it done. Being *accountable* means that you don't pass the buck. When something is your fault, you don't offer excuses—you offer solutions. Passing the buck is not part of the DNA of any winning team.

Coach Saunders also mentioned being *available,* which reminds me of a quote from Woody Allen: *"Showing up is 80 percent of life."* Looking back on my career in professional sports, there have been a lot of things that I've been fortunate to experience, such as being the quarterback of a championship team and being named MVP of the National Football League. Despite those achievements, the thing that I'm singularly most proud of is the fact that I showed up for work every day. I played 163 consecutive football games and never missed a day of practice. That's my idea of being available.

When it comes to being reliable, accountable, and available, almost nothing speaks to that more than how you approach being on time. I bet that every last one of you would rather work with someone who shows up on time over someone who is chronically late and comes armed with a variety of reasons why it's never his or her fault, as in: "Traffic was horrible," or "I overslept," or "The dog ate my watch."

I've always been a stickler for showing up on time. When you're late for something, it sends a message that you believe you are more important than everyone else and that the rules don't apply to you. It's also just downright rude. Showing up on time is what successful people do. If you're chronically late, change that behavior before you become known for being unreliable.

Root #4: Ability

Finally, we circle back to *ability*. Our abilities are the raw talents we possess, as well as the skills we have learned and developed. *Ability* is tangible. It's what we see when we first evaluate a person: how fast they can run, how high they can jump, and how quickly and efficiently they can process information.

These talents and skills are important; in fact, most of the time, ability is what opens the door to opportunity. But it's not what *keeps* the door open. That's up to your character, your willingness to learn, your work ethic, and your trustworthiness. And those are the traits that make the difference between an average team member and a highly valued team member. NBA superstar Michael Jordan said it best:

"Talent wins games, but teamwork and intelligence wins championships."

Many Cogs, One Wheel

Through his infinite wisdom, Coach Gibbs helped me understand many things—and one of them was deciphering the term *role*. At first glance, it's a simple word. It's commonplace. It has one tiny syllable. When you peel away the outer layer, however, there's a lot of substance in that four-letter word.

What role do you play in an organization? From time to time, it's helpful to reexamine your *real* role—not just the one on your business card—to ensure that you are making your presence known, making the most out of your position, and assigning a name, face, and specific talents to that role.

A while back, I noticed that the team members at my restaurant were not answering the phone in a way that spoke to the value of their roles. When you called Joe Theismann's Restaurant in Alexandria, Virginia, our associates would pick up the phone and say, "Hi, Joe Theismann's Restaurant, can I help you?"

I thought, What if someone came into our restaurant and there was confusion about their reservation? Our customers need to know whom they are talking to within our organization. So we had our team members make a minor change to their greeting. We asked them to simply add their names, as in, "Hi, Joe Theismann's Restaurant, this is Jimmy speaking. How can I help you?" It was a simple but powerful change.

Always identify yourself and your role. Doing so allows you to take more ownership in your position, and it breathes life into your title.

Understanding your role and being the best teammate you can be also means being willing to step into other roles for the good of the team. Take Troy Brown, who played for the New England Patriots for fifteen years, which is an eternity in pro football—and even more impressive when you consider that he spent his entire career with one team. One of the many reasons the Patriots never traded him had to do with more than just the talent he possessed in his official role as a slot receiver. He was willing to wear whatever hat was needed to be a part of the team.

When Troy was asked to play defensive back, he didn't hesitate for a second. As a matter of fact, in 2004, he had three interceptions. He could have walked up to Coach Belichick and said, "Hey, I'm not sure about this. It's not my role. It's not what you pay me to do." Instead, he took on the role because that's what his team needed, no questions asked.

 ## Are you willing to do whatever it takes to help your team?

Real champions, like Troy Brown, embody the saying, "There's no *I* in *team.*" And that's a much-needed antidote to a society that is constantly telling you to make something of *yourself.* Now, I agree with the idea of self-empowerment, which is why two of my favorite questions are, "What will it take for *you* to be a champion?" and "What makes *you* special?" However, if you believe that your successes are all because of *you,* you are woefully misguided. I once asked Troy Aikman—a three-time Super Bowl champion and Hall of Fame quarterback—what the one thing was that made him a champion, and here was his reply:

"What makes me special are the people around me."

Ineffective teams are those with team members who have their own agendas. It's a fatal flaw to have anyone on a team who doesn't give themselves unselfishly to the team. It comes back to what my friend Fred Paglia calls "subservience to a purpose." If the team buys into the purpose, it draws everyone around that one goal. Selfish acts are simply not tolerated on championship teams.

No matter our role, and no matter how important our job is to an organization, we are but a single cog in a very large wheel. And that's not a bad thing. If we were all truly irreplaceable, companies would fail left and right once people reached retirement age or otherwise left the company. So know your role, embrace it, and stay both humble and grateful for the opportunity to be a part of something greater than yourself—even if that means taking on a task that is not in your job description. Who knows? You may discover a hidden talent. At the very least, it will give you an appreciation for the role that someone else on your team plays.

Equality Equals Achievement

Traditionally, the quarterback is the most spotlighted position on the field. But a lot of people don't realize that it's also the single most *dependent* position. For instance, if the offensive line doesn't block, it's difficult for the quarterback to throw the ball. If the receivers don't catch, the quarterback will never get a completion. If kickers don't make kicks, it's really hard to win. (*Thank you, Mark Moseley, placekicker extraordinaire and MVP of the National Football League in 1982.*)

Just because a position is in the public eye or comes with a greater air of prestige, that doesn't mean it's more important. Whether you're the "quarterback" of your business or you're at the front desk answering the phone, no individual is greater than the team. Besides, most celebrated athletes and businesspeople didn't achieve great success by themselves. They had an idea. They made a plan. Then they trusted other people on the team to do their jobs.

When I'm speaking to a group, I like to ask the audience, "Who are some of the most vital people within your organization? Is it the CEO? Is it the CFO? What about the VP of human resources or the marketing director?" Yes, executives are important, but there are other people in the organization who also contribute to its success in vital ways. I personally believe that some of the most important people in an organization are the men and women who sit behind the front desk. These team members are on the front lines. They are critical to the team because they are often the ones who make the first impression with customers and clients.

Are the executives *less* important? No. Every member of the team has a specific and important role. If you are a teammate who is grounded by the four roots I just discussed—character, intelligence, work ethic, and ability—then no matter what your title may be, both your presence and your absence should be felt. It doesn't mean that you aren't replaceable, but it does mean that the proverbial team circle is incomplete without you.

One more Coach Gibbs story: In 1996, when Joe was inducted into the Pro Football Hall of Fame, I was fortunate enough to be in attendance at the ceremony. During his acceptance speech, he recognized the people who had helped give him the opportunity to be inducted into the Hall of Fame. As he named players, friends, and influencers, I thought, *I was his starting QB for six years and quarterbacked one of his championship teams. For sure, he's gonna mention me.*

While I sat there waiting to hear my name mentioned, Coach proceeded to single out just two players: Otis Wonsley and Reggie Branch. Otis was a running back on the kickoff coverage team, and Reggie was a blocking back in short yardage and goal-line situations. Great guys. Great role players. But as Coach concluded his speech without uttering my name, I thought, *What about me? What about Art Monk, John Riggins, or Darrell Green?*

Looking back, it wasn't my proudest moment. Thankfully, I finally passed through that foolish, recognition-seeking phase, and in hindsight, I realized what Coach Gibbs was saying.

There are guys on every team who are perceived as the "stars." But every member of his team, every last man that he coached—they were all responsible for what we achieved as a team and for him being inducted into the Hall of Fame.

I realized that every member of a team is significant in different but equal ways. When you start to think that your role is more important than the role of the man or woman sitting next to you, your team will never experience the powerful multiplier effect of a high-functioning team.

Taking People for Granted "Stinks"

You never want to wake up one day realizing that you took the things and the people around you for granted. One of my favorite examples of why taking people for granted is an unhealthy practice took place one cold December over thirty years ago. New York City's sanitation collectors had gone on strike in the heart of the holiday season, pulling almost 2,000 trash collectors from their duties on December 1, 1981. Within a few days, even the glow of the Christmas trees and twinkling lights could not distract from the filth that was piling up around the city.

On upscale Fifth Avenue, shoppers waded through mountains of stinking trash as they shopped for Christmas gifts. It was even worse in the neighborhoods in the outer boroughs; thousands of tons of garbage had piled up, creating hazardous conditions for both walking and driving. Traffic jams increased exponentially as people scurried into oncoming traffic to avoid the piles of waste building up on the sidewalks.

Then, on December 6, a strong windstorm sent five days of garbage hurling through the air across the city. According to Robert D. McFadden of the *New York Times*, "Everywhere, it seemed, waste paper was swirling and flying like tattered kites and garbage was tumbling and skittering along." Not long after, dozens of trash-fueled fires began to rage out of control.

Eight days into the strike, garbage was as high as the second floor of buildings, producing a stench so putrid that people entered their houses through back entrances to avoid it. Pretty soon, sewer rats (and their diseases) came topside by the tens of thousands to revel in the filth. In fact, had it not been cold outside, the situation would have developed into a serious health crisis.

The strike officially ended on December 17, and New Yorkers woke up a few days later to a wondrous holiday sight. It wasn't Santa Claus. It was their glorious sanitation workers, hauling away the foul accumulation that had turned New York City into a rotten wasteland.

Haven't thought about your sanitation experts lately? I bet you will now. You might even feel compelled to thank them the next time you see them hauling away your trash.

Now think about your workplace for a minute and about the little things you take for granted. Someone cleans the toilets and refills the paper towel dispenser. Someone restocks the vending machine. Someone delivers your mail. Someone makes the coffee. They are all part of the team.

 Make someone's day, simply by thanking them for something they have done. Recognition is simple but powerful.

No one is expecting you to throw a ticker tape parade for every last person on your team. But that's the thing about appreciation—it doesn't need to be elaborate. It just needs to *exist*. Simply slow down from time to time and be grateful for those around you. By performing their vital role on the team, they make it possible for you to perform yours.

Separating the Wheat from the Chaff

"Separating the wheat from the chaff" is an idiom that refers to the ancient practice of winnowing grain. It's an expression that's easy enough to interpret—the wheat is the solid, good stuff that is used to make flour, and the chaff must be removed before the wheat can be fully utilized. When people use the idiom today, it often refers to an event, trial, or process that identifies the elements within ourselves that must be removed before we can become true champions in life.

Bill Belichick is a man who knows what it takes to separate the wheat from the chaff and create winners, having won six World Championships as a head coach, as well as having coached in several others.

Having studied Bill's teams, it appears to me that he uses a philosophy that I refer to as E^3.

- E1: The first "e" is the *environment* that he creates for his staff and his players—and, really, for the entire organization. In the environment he creates, there are certain responsibilities that must be met. One of the unique aspects of his environment is that there's only one voice—his—that speaks to any issues about his football team.
- E2: The second "e" is the *expectations* that he places on himself and everyone in the organization. The New England Patriots don't start preparing for a season by thinking about winning a division or conference championship. Their expectation is to win the World Championship. Too often in life, we don't ask enough of ourselves and we don't ask enough of the people around us. Bill asks for both.
- E3: The third "e" is the *execution* that he expects on the field. You have to be able to perform at a championship level.

Hall of Fame coach Bill Parcells is another man who knows what it takes to create World Champions. Not only did Bill take four different teams to the playoffs (the Giants, Patriots, Jets, and Cowboys), but he also created a lasting, winning culture within each of the four organizations. What he did was quite unique, and he focused on doing things that separated the men from the boys. Bill seems to build cultures around a principle that I call D².

- D1: He provided his football teams with crystal clear *direction*. He told them where they were going to go and exactly what it was going to take to get there. Too much of the time, we operate without a clear direction, and that's how we end up disappointed and unsatisfied when we don't get the results we wanted. As Yogi Berra once said, "If you don't know where you're going, you might end up somewhere else."

  Bill spelled out his intended direction with extreme clarity by placing a major emphasis on practice. We've all heard that "practice makes perfect," and Bill Parcells's leadership style is the embodiment of that saying. The greatest leaders engrain the value of practice in their teams, just like Bill did.

  His emphasis on having a well-defined direction also led him to become known for being a clear-intentioned leader. None of his players ever had to guess where they stood in his eyes. Bill never let there be any doubt. Being honest isn't always the *easiest* policy, but Bill felt it was always the *best* policy for his teams.

- D2: Bill was also an extremely *detail-oriented* leader. He accentuated small points of emphasis to promote a team-wide focus on the minute details of the game. For example, if the Giants were getting ready to play the San Francisco 49ers, he would highlight every last detail about their opponents, point-by-point and player-by-player. He explained to his defense that the way they would see 49ers receiver Jerry Rice come off the ball on the first play would be the *exact* same way they'd see him come off the ball on the last play. That meant the defense had to pay close attention to every play, since those details could mean the difference between first and second place.

Bill was also highly detailed in the way he dealt with his players. He never lumped every team member into one category. Instead, he tailored his leadership and communication styles to each individual on the team. Bill was able to do this because he truly understood people. As a coach, he recognized that a gentle hand worked well with one player, while a firmer hand worked better with another. Knowing how to relate to each individual member of the team is a key attribute of all great leaders.

Living and working according to the D^2 principle is not easy—but what great accomplishment is easy? The greatest payoffs in life require some risk. Bill Parcells believed that winners were the ones who were not afraid to take a chance, and so he encouraged his players to take the "road less traveled" by choosing to undertake some risk— and that's one of the reasons Bill is in the Hall of Fame today.

 Valuable team players are prepared to make sacrifices for the greater good.

Speaking of tough, road-less-taken actions, over the years I've discovered a few others that most people find hard to do. But they also happen to be the things that turn ordinary teams into champions, and are the activities that separate the victors from everybody else.

1. Take One for the Team

Ever wonder where the phrase "take one for the team" came from? It originates from baseball. A batter "takes one for the team" by allowing himself to be hit by a pitch in order to freely advance to first base. It may be painful, but the batter is willing to do it because it results in an advantage for the team. Today, the phrase has evolved into the notion of making a sacrifice of any kind in order to give your team (of any kind) an advantage.

Roger Craig was a great Hall of Fame running back who played for the San Francisco 49ers during most of the 1980s. I once asked Roger, "What's the one thing that made you a champion?" He explained that he strived to be the best play-faking running back in the National Football League. He wanted his opponents to be absolutely convinced that he had the ball, even though he didn't. His reasoning was simple: If he could convince the defense that he had the ball, they'd all be trying to tackle him, making it easier for Joe Montana to throw the ball to Jerry Rice.

This was the epitome of taking one for the team, which really boils down to being unselfish. You shouldn't always be the person who takes one for the team but acting unselfishly is one of the best ways to build trust and create the kinds of bonds that inspire and propel your team to greatness.

2. Choose a Successor

Mike Tomlin, the coach of the Pittsburgh Steelers, talks about a philosophy that has become a guiding credo for his players and his coaching staff: *Teach the man behind you to take your job.*

You may be thinking, *Why would I want someone to take my job?* That's a great question, but before I answer, let me ask you an important question:

Are you going to live forever?

Someday, someone else will be doing your job.

Chuck Pagano was the head coach of the Indianapolis Colts, but a few years ago, he wasn't sure that he would be for much longer. Pagano was diagnosed with a form of leukemia in September 2012, which necessitated an indefinite leave of absence from his coaching duties. One of his assistant coaches, Bruce Arians, became interim head coach of the Colts. Bruce took over in a seamless transition and led the Colts to a 9–3 record the remainder of that year.

This was one of the biggest one-season turnarounds in NFL history. The nine wins are also the most victories won by an interim head coach in NFL history, which earned him the title of AP NFL Head Coach of the Year in 2012. In 2013, Bruce was named head coach of the Arizona Cardinals, and in 2014, after posting an 11–5 record, he was once again named AP NFL Head Coach of the Year. (He is currently head coach of the Tampa Bay Buccaneers.)

Arians is a heck of a coach in his own right, but what enabled him to step into the position with virtually no hiccups was the fact that they had a succession plan in place. Perhaps even more notable was that Chuck was able to step aside and put his complete trust in someone else, so that he could take care of a higher priority—his health. And fortunately, after three months of treatment, doctors announced that his cancer was in remission. The following season, Chuck resumed his position as head coach in Indianapolis.

When it comes to being the best team member and leader you can be, you have to decide who's going to take over when you leave and how you will ensure that they aren't left reinventing the wheel. Why not give your successors and the rest of your team the greatest chance at future success?

In 2011, when Steve Jobs stepped down from his role as the leader of Apple, and then tragically passed away later that year, the sustainability of Apple's phenomenal success without its visionary leader was in serious question for investors and consumers alike.

But Jobs had been grooming then COO Tim Cook to take over since 2004, when Cook had temporarily stepped into the role of CEO while Jobs was recovering from pancreatic cancer.

When Jobs chose Cook as his successor, he offered two pieces of advice, which speaks to the kind of man and leader Steve Jobs was at his core. As Alyssa Newcomb of ABC News recounted the story, Jobs told Cook not to think of what he would do, and to "do what's right." If it weren't for Jobs's foresight to prepare the way for his successor, Apple might not still be the trailblazer it is today. Jobs himself said it best as he stepped down: "I believe Apple's brightest and most innovative days are ahead of it."

Apple remains a forward-thinking technology juggernaut and continues to stay one step ahead of the competition because Jobs knew that even the greatest, most pioneering leaders must have a succession plan in place.

3. Pick the Right Horse

One of the mistakes I see in business is picking the wrong person for the job. Have you ever heard of a company taking their top salesperson and promoting that person to manager? Although some salespeople may make good leaders, sales talent doesn't inherently translate into managerial ability. The company has potentially weakened *two* positions as opposed to strengthening one.

If you want to have a real chance of winning the race, you have to pick the right horse. It's the same in sports—you don't want a 5'9" 185-pound running back trying to block a 6'6" 300-pound defensive lineman. When it comes to your business, making sure that you have the right people doing the right things is an imperative for championship-caliber teams.

4. Do Things That Others Don't (or Won't)

If you work for a large company, you've likely never met the leader of your organization. Yet it's imperative for leaders to connect with the people they work with at all levels. And most team members would consider it a true honor to personally meet the CEO or president. Imagine that you work the third shift at a large manufacturing plant, and the CEO stops by one evening, introduces him- or herself, and thanks you for the work that you're doing. Chances are, it would make you feel proud and a valued part of the team, and you'd probably tell your family about it as soon as you got home.

Special leaders go above and beyond for their teams. They do the little things that make a big difference, like expressing gratitude to their employees.

In addition to putting in the effort themselves, championship team leaders also ask their team to do the things that no one else is doing. One of my favorite examples of this is from the former president of real estate powerhouse RE/MAX, Margaret Kelly. When she was leading the company, Margaret designated days where no one in the office was allowed to send an email or text to anyone else in the office. If an employee wanted to have a conversation with a fellow team member, he or she had to get up, seek that person out, and sit down face-to-face to discuss the matter.

It's amazing how many people lose touch with the individuals sitting right next to them. So much more is conveyed when we sit down with one another, as opposed to sending a text or email. This is why I believe more companies should incorporate simple team-building activities into their culture—actions that remind us that some of the most important people in the world are literally within arm's reach.

If you want to learn even more about how a winning team operates, there's a great book called *Everybody Wins: The Story and Lessons Behind RE/MAX* by Phil Harkins and Keith Hollihan. It digs into how RE/MAX has achieved such phenomenal success and how the company has become what it is today. Specifically, it examines the company's strategy, team culture, and leadership— all of which was instilled by the vision that its founder, Dave Liniger, and his wife, Gail, had for the company.

The Hallmark of True Team Leadership

You've probably heard of Chesley B. "Sully" Sullenberger—he is the captain who famously landed US Airways Flight 1549 in the Hudson River after their Airbus A320 flew through a flock of birds so massive that the impact disabled both engines. Not only did he land the plane safely in near-freezing water, he also didn't lose a single passenger or crew member. His accomplishment is what has become known as the "Miracle on the Hudson."

Captain Sullenberger received tremendous accolades for his heroic actions, but those closest to him say that he is one of the humblest men they know. He personifies what it means to be a selfless leader. He was honored in the media, and he was even invited to the Presidential Inauguration Ceremony by President-Elect Barack Obama on January 20, 2009. But while Captain Sullenberger appreciated the invitation, he explained that he couldn't attend alone, and that every member of the crew had to be there at his side. To me, that is real leadership, and that is what a real team attitude looks like. Leaders who recognize and understand that it's not all about them are the ones whose legacies live on forever.

The debate over whether true leaders are *born* or *made* could go on and on. Regardless, I believe that within all of us exists the capacity for great leadership. But as with all the best things in life, getting there isn't easy.

Anyone can manage. Management is about *compliance*. But leadership is about *engagement*. The leaders who focus on the locker room (in other words, the working environment) as much as they focus on the game plan are the ones who are the most successful.

There are three doctrines that championship teams and their leaders live by and embrace that set themselves apart. Even if you aren't a "born leader," you can be well on your way to becoming a trusted, respected, and highly valued team member by incorporating these three principles into your business and life:

1. Know What You Don't Know

Admitting that you don't have all the answers is not something that comes naturally to all leaders. If you think you have all the answers, I'll let you in on a little secret: *You probably don't know as much as you think you know.* No one does. The best leaders are comfortable knowing that it's not about being the smartest person in the room; it's about being the most effective team possible. As Donald Rumsfeld said: "As we know, there are known knowns; there are things we know we know. We also know there are known unknowns; that is to say, we know there are some things we do not know."

Art Markman wrote a fascinating article in the *Harvard Business Review*, "Do You Know What You Don't Know?" In the article he recounts a corporate meeting he attended where "the vice president spoke about streamlining business practices in the coming year. During the talk, executives around the room nodded in agreement. Afterward, though, many of them discussed what *streamlining* actually meant. None of the people who had nodded in agreement could exactly define the mechanics of how to streamline a business practice." The vice president never explained how or what the streamlining of the business practices would be.

Admitting what you don't know requires both strength and humility.

Do you know what you *don't* know? Egos, pride, and other human tendencies prevent a lot of us from asking for the help we need to lead a team or be a better team member. However, when you do ask for help, the results can be remarkable. Coach Joe Gibbs was not only the head coach but a tremendous offensive coach, yet he didn't understand our defense as well. However, he knew what he didn't know, which is why he brought in a coach by the name of Richie Petitbon to be his defensive coordinator. At that time, Richie was considered one of the top coordinators in football. Head coaches have so much on their plate that it is virtually impossible to know all three phases of football and run the team, because each unit is different and has different responsibilities. Joe recognized his strength was handling the offense and knew he needed someone who was capable of handling the defense.

Because of Joe's willingness to recognize what he didn't know, the 1983 Washington Redskins had an unheard-of giveaway/takeaway ratio (also known as a plus/minus ratio or turnover margin) that year. Takeaway and giveaway statistics really speak to the strength of a team's defense. As a general rule, teams that have more takeaways than their opposition tend to have a better chance of winning, since they have more opportunities to score than the other team.

The 1983 Washington Redskins had a plus/minus ratio of plus-43. To give you an idea of how impressive that is, the average plus/minus ratio of *all past Super Bowl winners* is plus-8.7. It was truly an incredible football team with an extraordinary defense. And it was all because Coach Gibbs recognized that his strength wasn't defense but that he could ask for help from someone who *did* possess that strength.

You have to know what you don't know. And you can't be afraid to bring in other people who possess a skill set or area of expertise that is simply not in your wheelhouse. I love what John C. Maxwell says about leadership: "Leadership is not about titles, positions, or flowcharts. It is about one life influencing another."

2. All for One, One for All

I once had the honor of playing in a golf tournament in Camp Lejeune, North Carolina, alongside a young man named Joey Bozik. Joey is a retired Army sergeant who served our country in Iraq. There are some physical characteristics about Joey that you don't often see on the golf course—Joey is a triple amputee. Both of his legs are gone from the knee down, most of one arm is gone from the elbow down, and his remaining arm operates at about 70 percent capacity.

After we played a few holes, I asked Joey what happened. What he told me will stay with me forever. First, he explained how he lost his limbs. He was working security in Iraq in 2004 with the Army military police when his Humvee rolled over a bomb. The injuries to the driver and the gunner riding with him that day weren't life-threatening, but Bozik's were.

Then Joey made a comment that blew me away. He said, "Even though I'm in the situation I'm in, I can live with it, because the men that I was responsible for are okay."

Being responsible for those we lead is leadership.

I recently discovered that Joey has taken to mastering other sports besides golf. Mark Francescutti wrote an article titled "Battling All Odds" in the *Dallas Morning News* about Joey's progress: Without the use of prosthetics, Joey now competes in the martial art of Brazilian jiu-jitsu. When asked about his ability to take on "able-bodied" men, Joey said, "Don't put yourself out of it before you get into it. Never give up. There's always a way if you're willing to try."

That's the kind of person who inspires his or her team and bonds them together with a force that is stronger than steel.

Another inspiring military leader is Lieutenant Colonel Hal Moore. Colonel Moore is best known as the commander of the 1st Battalion, 7th Cavalry Regiment, at the Battle of Ia Drang, during the Vietnam War in 1965. He is famous for inspiring his men through heroic words and actions. In the book *We Were Soldiers Once . . . And Young*, which he co-authored with Joseph Galloway (the only journalist on the ground throughout the fighting), Moore wrote these words:

> In the American Civil War, it was a matter of principle that a good officer rode his horse as little as possible. There were sound reasons for this. If you are riding and your soldiers are marching, how can you judge how tired they are, how thirsty, how heavy their packs weigh on their shoulders?

That way of thinking—which stems from a desire to connect with your team, build trust, and encourage teamwork—is one of many things that made Lt. Col. Moore such an exemplary leader. It comes down to a single force at work, which brings us back to the words of another great military mind, General Colin Powell, from his "Leadership Primer" presentation. It summarizes the powerful effect that leaders like Lt. Col. Moore and Sgt. Bozik have on their teams, something that General Powell calls "*perpetual optimism.*"

PERPETUAL OPTIMISM IS A FORCE MULTIPLIER

The ripple effect of a leader's enthusiasm and optimism is awesome. So is the impact of cynicism and pessimism. Leaders who whine and blame engender those same behaviors among their colleagues. I am not talking about stoically accepting organizational stupidity and performance incompetence with a "What, me worry?" smile. I am talking about a gung-ho attitude that says, "We can change things here; we can achieve awesome goals; we can be the best." Spare me the grim litany of the "realist"; give me the unrealistic aspirations of the optimist any day.

I've heard story after story of military leaders who exemplified that kind of "team first" attitude, which is one of the things that makes our United States military the greatest team in the entire world. All teams—business, athletic, or otherwise—could learn some valuable lessons from the examples set by our military men and women in uniform.

3. The Whole Is Greater Than the Sum of Its Parts

Who hasn't had a Big Mac from McDonald's at some point in his or her life? You may even be the kind of person who occasionally gets a "Big Mac Attack." What many don't realize is that the Golden Arches' signature sandwich was invented far away from McDonald's research and development department at their headquarters. It was actually invented in 1967 by an early franchise owner in Pittsburgh named Jim Delligatti. The nationwide introduction of the sandwich in 1968 increased McDonald's sales by 12 percent, and at forty-five cents, they sold it for twice as much as any hamburger.

The famous menu item was created by a team member out in the field—a man who was in touch with customers on a daily basis. And Delligatti's invention was all made possible through an idea called *participatory management*, which is the practice of empowering employees to participate in organizational decision-making. The Big Mac changed the menu of the largest fast-food chain in the world because one franchisee was empowered by his company to think outside the box and be a contributing member of the team.

Empower the people who you work with to be creative. They are the ones out in the field. They are the ones fighting the battles. They are the ones doing the things to help the company grow. They are powerful sources of information. So utilize the resources of your team by empowering its members. It really all comes down to a simple idea:

$$1 + 1 = 3$$

That's not bad math. It's a concept called *synergy*, which is defined as the creation of a whole that is greater than the sum of its parts. It's the concept that makes teamwork so powerful. The term *synergy* comes from the Greek verb *synergazomai*, meaning "to work together." When two or more people come together, the results achieved by the "sum of the parts" can literally be exponential compared to the actions of the "parts" on their own.

Empower people! Ask them to step outside their personal silos and give them the opportunity to figure out ways to help their companies grow. They are not the first line of *defense* (being reactive), but the first line of *offense* (being proactive). It's about making your people feel like more than a number. While they may be one of many in the organization, they should have no doubt in their minds that you not only desire to hear what they have to say, but that you *need* to hear what they have to say.

Let them know that you believe they *can* and *will* make a difference.

BONUS #5

Good Advice Is Worthless Unless
You Listen, Consider, and Act on It

WHEN I PLAYED PROFESSIONAL football, I had an agent help me negotiate all of my contracts—except for my last one. When it came time to negotiate my contract in 1984, I dealt directly with Redskins owner Jack Kent Cooke. I traveled to his rolling farmlands in Virginia, anticipating a discussion about the particulars of my contract. But when I got there, we didn't discuss the contract. He wasn't ready yet. Instead, we took a leisurely ride on two of his Tennessee walking horses. Afterward, I drove home, still wondering about my future.

Later, I made the trip to Mr. Cooke's house for what would be the final time. As I sat down at the desk in his round house, Mr. Cooke sat across from me and placed a large binder between us. He opened the binder, and I read the amount of my new contract. I'd had a certain number in mind, and he actually exceeded that number.

Using common negotiating sense, I didn't say a word. Mr. Cooke broke the silence. "Well, what do you think?"

"This is terrific," I replied. What more could I say?

Mr. Cooke looked at me and made an important correction, in true Jack Kent Cooke style. He said, "Nooooooo, it is not. It is *fabulous!*"

There were no incentive clauses built into the contract, meaning that I wouldn't get a bonus for things like winning the division or being named MVP. But the base salary of over a million dollars a year for five years was already more than I'd hoped for, *including* any incentives. That amount may not seem as impressive by today's professional football salary standards, but in 1984, that was a significant deal.

Mr. Cooke continued, "You've proven to me that you don't need bonuses or incentives to be motivated to play the game."

Then he offered a nugget of advice. "Joe, I want you to *insure* this contract."

To which I replied, "I've played for you for eleven years. You know I'm going to show up."

Jack shook his head. "It's not for me. Joe, you insure this contract because it is a *prudent business decision.*"

He gave me the contact information for an insurance agent from Lloyd's of London. Then he said, "And, Joe, do not deduct the payment for the premiums of this policy from your taxes. That way, if something does happen, that money comes back *net* to you."

I took his advice and insured my contract. Then I wrote a $35,000 check. Sure enough, a short time later, Mr. Cooke's wisdom changed my life. My career was over with a single *snap.* But because I had that policy and had not written it off, I was able to start my life after football in a financially sound way.

If you're a golfer, have you insured your hand? If you're a ballerina, have you insured your feet? And, of course, it's not just athletes who need to make sound insurance decisions. Do you have policies in place that will ensure that your family will be well taken care of should something happen to you or your ability to make a living?

Part of being a champion is staying open to hearing critical pieces of business and financial advice from others. One moment's worth of advice can make a lifetime of difference. Keep your ears and your mind open to the wisdom of those around you. Consider it. Act on it.

"Every engine has something that turns it on.
You be the ignitor in your life."

6

MOTIVATION
Uncover What Compels You to Win

That thing that enables greatness is
the champion that exists within us all.

"Someday" Is Today

Let's be honest—it's a whole lot easier to *not* work hard and just
let life happen. It's incredibly easy to allow years of your life to
pass by while justifying your decisions to avoid unpleasant or hard
work. And when it comes to finding reasons why putting off a task
is the *right thing* to do, most of us are highly skilled at it.

"My desk is such a mess. I'll spend today getting really orga-
nized, and then tomorrow, I'll start working."

Motivation is what enables us to do what we'd rather not do.
Motivation also pulls the blinders off our eyes and helps us realize,
"Do I really need to clean my desk? Or am I afraid that I'll do the
wrong kind of work? Or worse, that I'll work hard, only to fail?"

Most of us genuinely want to feel better, look better, and have
better things in life. However, too few of us take responsibility for
motivating ourselves when it comes to making the necessary

changes that get us on the road to "better." Why? It's because be-coming better versions of ourselves is no easy task. It takes months, years, or sometimes a lifetime to get to where we ultimately want to be.

True and lasting motivation comes from managing your mind and your emotions. If you can succeed at doing that, you'll dis-cover what makes you tick, which in turn allows you to manage your actions in a more productive way. If you fail to manage your mind, you will be destined to live a life filled with regret and a quiet desperation.

In other words, you'll always be a "someday" person.

When you hear a child begin a sentence with "Someday, I'll . . ." it's exciting, because you know they are envisioning big things for their future. But when you hear an adult utter "Someday, I'll . . ." there is almost nothing more depressing.

Understand that there is no someday. *Someday is today.* And, yes, there could be something, someone, or some feeling that is hold-ing you back from doing "someday" actions today. But it's up to *you* to find the motivating factors that will enable you to press on and fight the good fight.

We're all unique, and there are an endless number of motivat-ing factors that can nudge each of us in the right direction. How-ever, for the most part, I've found that there are nine influencers that form the true bedrock of motivation. They are the fundamen-tal motivators that allow us to take the opportunities we are pre-sented with in life and turn them into something great.

 What gets you out of bed in the morning and lights the fire inside you?

In this chapter, I'll briefly examine each of those nine motivators and share ideas about how you can identify the motivator that best suits your needs. I'll also help you figure out the right goals to get you there. The motivators in this chapter are not listed in any particular order of importance, since the *formula* for the fuel that lights each of our fires is a little different. As you read, ask yourself which combination of motivators gets you out of bed in the morning. And then use that combination to propel yourself upward and onward every day.

1. Money Moves Us

When it comes to motivators, money is the most obvious impetus for action. Money buys the food, shelter, and clothing that we need to live. You work to put a roof over your head and to support your family. Of course, money can also buy far more than that. Healthy bank accounts lead to nice cars, big houses, lavish vacations, and all the other things that physically represent success.

Money motivates—there's just no getting around it. But money can't be the only reason you choose to act. It can't be the only reason you get out of bed. There has to be more to life than the almighty dollar.

If you make a lot of money doing something you despise, or something that compromises your character, what's the point? Some people may think, *I'll just suffer through this job because it pays well.* That's a nice idea in theory, but here's a reality check:

Every day, you are one day closer to your last day on earth. You know that day you just spent doing something you despise? You're never going to get it back. It's gone forever.

Why spend another day doing something that makes you unhappy? Life is too precious, and you are far too valuable to live your life devoid of that opportunity. Money can provide status, the ability to acquire more stuff, and a certain amount of freedom. But it doesn't buy happiness. If you need proof, just ask some of the world's biggest lottery winners. A sudden infusion of a large amount of money into your life has a name—it's called the "Lottery Curse." It's a designation given to the profoundly negative effects that new-found riches often have on the lives of lottery winners.

It's normal, even necessary, to pursue financial security—*but bear in mind the cost of that pursuit.* There has to be a love for what you do. There has to be a passion for what you are pursuing in order for you to get out of your warm bed, face rush-hour traffic, and spend more hours away from your family than you spend with them. If you have to make those kinds of sacrifices, you should be able to answer *yes*, without hesitation, when someone asks, "Is it really worth it?"

While money is a motivating factor, and we need it to survive, it can't be the sole reason for doing the things you do. Ideally, money should be a by-product of loving what you're doing and being great at it.

2. Pride in Our Work Keeps Us Going

The word *pride* often has a negative connotation. It's considered the original and most deadly of the seven deadly sins. But the kind of pride I'm referring to is not the kind that involves excessive personal admiration or a disregard for the accomplishments of others. I'm talking about an *inspiring kind of pride*—a satisfied sense of attachment toward one's own choices and actions, or to-ward an entire group of people or organization. It is a positive product of self-reflection and a fulfilled feeling of belonging. And it's one of the most powerful motivators in the world.

During my time with the Redskins, I played alongside place-kicker Mark Moseley, who happens to be the only special teams player who has ever won the title of NFL MVP. Mark was meticu-lous when it came to his uniform and his appearance—as a matter of fact, he's still that way today. On one particularly rainy, cold November day in 1980, we were playing the Philadelphia Eagles. Before the game, I walked up to a mirror to perform my pregame ritual of applying eye black. I knew that on a dark, rainy day, eye black wouldn't serve much of a purpose, but I never messed with my routine. I'm just too superstitious.

As I applied the eye black, Mark stood beside me, looking into the mirror as he fixed his hair. He had been there for quite some time before I got there, and he was still styling his hair when I was done.

There I was, wondering how much longer he was going to spend styling his hair for a football game. I didn't want to interrupt him as he was going through his routine. But I was surprised at how long it was taking him, especially in light of the fact that it was pouring rain, and he'd be donning a helmet as soon as we left the locker room.

I approached it by starting a casual conversation. "Mark, it's raining out."

Mark replied, "Yeah, it's raining pretty hard out there."

I said, "You plan on wearing a helmet today?"

He replied, "Oh yeah, I'm going to wear a helmet."

I said, "Okay. Well then why are you fixing your hair?"

Without taking his eyes off the mirror or even glancing in my direction, he replied, *"I'm proud of who I am, and I'm proud of what I represent. Now hand me the hairspray."*

Those words have had a profound effect on the way I approach my actions and the way I represent myself. When you step out into the world, you're not just representing yourself. You are also representing your organization and your family through your words and actions. Be proud of who you are—and more importantly, take pride in what you represent, be it your organization, your family, or your own personal brand.

3. Positive Peer Pressure Pushes People

Peer pressure is another term that's gotten some bad publicity over the years, especially when it comes to younger generations. When used properly, however, positive peer pressure can be another highly effective motivator. Take a look at those sitting around you at work, and ask yourself, "Where do I fit in with these individuals?" I'm not just talking about the official capacities of your role. I'm talking about the real contributions you make and your ability to stand out from the crowd.

Next, ask yourself, "What kind of job is each person in my workplace doing?" Do the people around you underachieve or overachieve? Being among a group of overachievers can be intimidating, but it can also push you to greater heights. You are constantly being compared to those around you—and whether or not you measure up is entirely up to you.

Why do you think organizations have annual meetings where the best of the best in the company are recognized? Why do you think sports leagues give the title of MVP to the best player at the end of a season? It creates a desire in others to win those titles and accolades. It applies positive peer pressure.

Other people's successes often drive us to pursue our own. If you strive to overperform and become the best, just be aware that there is an increased pressure to live up to that elevated status going forward. But with the right emphasis, peer pressure can produce a powerful energy that becomes fuel for champions.

4. Recognition Fuels the Fire

When combined, the words "thank" and "you" are two of the sweetest words in the English language. Who doesn't love getting a pat on the back or receiving heartfelt thanks? We like to feel appreciated—it's the essence of who we are as human beings. That's the reason I handwrite thank-you letters to clients and

friends. We all want our work and accomplishments to be acknowledged and appreciated, and we want the little things that we
do in life to be valued.

 **Never underestimate the power of
combining the words "thank" and "you."**

A little recognition really does fuel the fire. In late November
of 1992, John Riggins and I were at RFK Stadium to be inducted
into the Washington Redskins Ring of Fame. The Ring of Fame is
a small group of players, coaches, and individuals who are honored with a plaque in the stadium (which is currently displayed at
FedExField).

There I stood on the fifty-yard line, in my suit and tie, waiting
for John to join me for the ceremony, which was scheduled
during halftime of that day's Redskins-Eagles game. John was no-
where to be seen, and I was starting to get antsy. Johnny was always quite the character, but this was not a good time for him to
show up late.

As I grew more impatient, so did the crowd. Then, all of a sudden, the crowd erupted into applause. I looked around and saw
what was causing the commotion. John had come bursting out
into the stadium in full battle regalia. He had on his #44 jersey,
along with the giant shoulder pads, thigh pads, and kneepads,
and his helmet was tucked under his arm.

The stadium exploded—people were screaming, yelling, and
cheering. Johnny jogged up to stand next to me. As I looked at
him in awe, I said, "John, you really are something."

He said, "Yes, I am, aren't I?"

Then I asked him one of my favorite questions: "Why? Why did
you do this?"

He said, "I had to hear it one more time."

I'd been gone seven years from the game, and John, having retired the year after me, had been gone for six. For six years, no one had cheered him on or made that "diesel" sound when John "The Diesel" Riggins carried the football. For six years, no one had cheered his touchdowns. For six years, he hadn't been able to take a bow.

He just had to hear it one more time.

Recognition really is that powerful. And it works both ways. John needed to hear the fans cheer, but I believe the fans also needed to say *thank you* one last time.

Recognition isn't just for the field, though, of course. It's also especially important at home. It's vitally important for parents to let their kids know that they're doing a great job and make it known how proud they are of them and their accomplishments.

If we continue to recognize kids and remind them that they're special, they're going to believe it. And if they believe they're doing great things, they'll continue to do great things.

Unfortunately, the converse of this is also true. If you criticize or try to mold kids into something they're not, they will grow up feeling that they will never be good enough. While feelings of inadequacy *might* make them try harder, most of the time, it simply makes them give up.

One of the biggest challenges I've seen in parenting is being able to give your children the freedom to pursue their own dreams. If you had a particular aspiration that was never realized, you might see the potential for realizing that dream in your children. But be careful not to push your dreams on them.

If you constantly push your kids in the direction *you* want them to travel, your kids will lose sight of the direction they had in mind for their own lives. Instead of pushing them, stand *beside* them. Allow them to fall, and then help them pick themselves back up. Recognize their special talents, and then give them room to develop those talents in the way *they* see fit. It's the most effective way to help your kids keep their eyes on the road ahead.

5. A Sense of Belonging Inspires

A *sense of belonging* may not be a type of motivation you've ever considered. To feel like you belong to something greater than yourself sounds nice—but can it really motivate? I'm here to tell you that it can. I've seen it. I've experienced it (and the lack of it) myself.

Bill Romanowski, or Romo, as he is often called, was a great linebacker who played for a number of teams throughout his career. He started with the San Francisco 49ers, then played with the Philadelphia Eagles and the Denver Broncos, and he finished his career as an Oakland Raider in 2002 and 2003. In 2002, I sat down with Bill before a Raiders game. During the course of the conversation, I asked him, "What's it been like for you coming to Oakland?"

"Well, Joe," he began, "it's really interesting . . ." Then he told me about his journey to finding a place where he felt he truly belonged. Romo had been unhappy in Denver. But when he came to Oakland, he was at peace once again. He struggled to understand why he had been so discontented in the Mile High City. Why did it make any difference what team he was on when football and a paycheck were all that really mattered?

Eventually, he came to realize that it wasn't the money that motivated him, and it wasn't the glory of the position he played. For him, his driving motivation came from having a sense of belonging.

Romo had been playing the game since 1988. When he moved to Denver for the start of the 1996 season, he didn't connect with the younger players who were part of the "gamer" generation—their idea of hanging out was playing video games. Romo had been used to the camaraderie of teammates who enjoyed going out and spending time with one another. But when he made the move to Oakland, he discovered an older group of players to whom he felt he could better relate. And that's when the game changed for him. He had found a sense of belonging again.

Before I broke my leg in 1985, I felt that same sense of belonging in Washington. But when I walked back into the locker room just weeks after my injury, that sense of belonging was gone. It was a devastating feeling. Whether on a field, in a workplace, or in any other environment, I believe that each of us wants to feel like we are exactly where we belong. And when we don't get that feeling, we chase it—like a dog chasing its tail.

Find where you fit in. When you do, you may discover a new-found motivation that comes with knowing that the pieces fit together.

And when the environment around you changes, don't be too quick to make yourself the outcast. Just because change happens, it doesn't automatically mean that you will no longer fit with the culture. With new generations always comes change. Inevitably, someday, you're going to be one of the "veterans" of your workplace. Do yourself, your family, and your organization a favor, and be willing to adapt. If a new technology is introduced, try it before you dismiss it as "ridiculous and unnecessary." The only thing that's ridiculous is being unwilling to accept the inevitable change that comes with the ebbs and flows of life.

 Finding your place in this world can become a powerful driving force.

6. Validation Can Be a Lifelong Pursuit

I've mentioned the concept of *validation* throughout this book. That's because the pursuit of validation has been a lifelong quest in my life. But I never used to think of it as a motivating factor. It wasn't until I grew older that I realized that wanting to *prove* to people that I belong was a tremendous and constant motivator for me.

I have traced the roots of my pursuit of validation back to my teenage years. After I chose to play for the Fighting Irish during my senior year in high school in 1967, my decision made the headline of a New Jersey newspaper. Here was the gist of the headline:

SKINNY KID THEISMANN WILL
GET SLAUGHTERED AT BIG NOTRE DAME

If you want to get me motivated, tell me I *can't* do something. Ever since reading that headline, whether out of spite, pride, or some combination of both, seeking validation and subsequently proving myself became a driving source of motivation. And it was all because somebody believed I didn't have what it took to be successful.

The need for validation has played a significant role throughout my football career. At the University of Notre Dame, I sought validation during all of my athletic performances, especially during games against our archrival, the University of Southern California (USC). I felt that if I played well against them, I *deserved* to be a college quarterback. When I joined the world of professional football, my new validation target became the Dallas Cowboys. If I played well against the Cowboys—who were the barometer of excellence in the game—then I *deserved* to be a professional quarterback.

Here's the thing, though. The best validation actually comes from *within*. It goes back to pride.

Even though you may continue to seek validation for some aspects of your life, believing you are special is up to *you*—not your spouse, your partner, your boss, or a newspaper headline. It took me close to a lifetime to realize that. Hopefully, I've saved you a few years of trying to figure out that lesson on your own.

7. Fear Has Its Place in the World

There's no question that fear can be a motivator. Reggie White, the great 6'5", 300-pound defensive end of the Green Bay Packers, could run a forty-yard dash in about 4.6 seconds. I could run that same distance in 5 seconds flat. You might assume that if Reggie was chasing me, he'd catch me—and based on the numbers alone, you'd be right. But if fear was a motivator, I'd summon my inner sprinter in that single instance and run it in 4.5 seconds.

Fear can be powerful, especially when used at the right moment. Author C. JoyBell C. says, "Don't be afraid of your fears. They're not there to scare you, they're there to let you know that something is worth it." We've all heard those accounts of a mother who was able to pick up the bumper of a car because her child was trapped underneath it. The feats that lie inside of us are incredible. Sometimes, fear is one of the greatest motivators to unearth our potential for greatness.

Every time I make any kind of public appearance, I get nervous. I'm not nervous because I'm scared; I'm nervous because I want to do a great job for the people who have invited me to be there. I'll never forget a discussion I had with Joe Montana, a Hall of Famer and a World Champion, that really put fear in perspective. During our conversation, he said:

"If you're not afraid to lose, then losing means nothing."

Fear really is powerful. In fact, it's so powerful that *fear as motivation* should never be seen as a long-term strategy. Much like the adrenaline it produces, fear is temporary. It's fleeting. If you rely on fear as your primary source of motivation, you'll find yourself both disappointed and exhausted—not to mention that it can eventually become a demotivator. Fear is also often the force that causes us to procrastinate, which is why it's best to use fear as a supplement to your foundational, more positive motivations.

8. Competition Carves Out Winners

We are a nation of people who love to compete. Competition allows us to satisfy that need that many of us have to win. It provides an opportunity and a reason for improving our performance. It motivates us to put forth greater effort and gives us something to aim for.

I guess you could call me a competition junkie. When I was playing football, every Monday morning, I would wake up wanting to know what other quarterbacks were doing— quarterbacks like Joe Montana, Dan Fouts, Ron Jaworski, and Roger Staubach—so that I could compare my stats to theirs. In my eyes, they were the competition. Their efforts and achievements became a benchmark for my own.

Competition starts during childhood, from how expertly we toss a ball to how well we can add and subtract. As we mature, we compete with siblings, students, and others for opportunities to play on the school team, get into college, or even date certain people. For those of you who are currently in a relationship, think back to your single days. It's Friday night, and you're competing for the attention of the lady or the gentleman you've been pining after—but all the while, you're probably also keeping tabs on the competition. Young ladies eye the competition, and men do the same. It's just how we are wired.

Some contests and events in life are, and should be, conducted specifically to determine "the winner." However, in situations where everyone on your team must contribute his or her best, success is not achieved by proclaiming one winner and the rest losers. Competition among those working toward a common goal may not always be wise. Use competition to spur you on but remember who you are competing against. And make sure that the competition within your team at work or on the field does not impede the progress of the team as a whole.

 Allow competition to sharpen you, but don't lose sight of the team's agenda in the pursuit of your own.

9. Live a Life Worth Living

At the beginning of the chapter, I mentioned that these motivators are not listed in any order of importance. If they had been, this last one would have been at the top of the list, written in bold, with gold stars beside it. This final stimulus has become my real reason for waking up in the morning. It encourages me to plant my feet on the ground and keeps me pressing on through each and every day.

I want to live a life worth living.

I've been lucky enough to enjoy many successes in my life. But I've realized something after all that success: It was always about what Joe Theismann did to get there. I thought that I wanted to be successful so that I could be on television shows, be in movies, and write books. I wanted it all for me, myself, and I, and my sense of validation came from beating the competition and receiving accolades.

It hit me the day I was in Memphis, Tennessee, visiting St. Jude Children's Research Hospital. The children there struggle with horrific diseases, and their families fight a far greater battle than I could ever imagine. Up until that point, it had been all about how many material things I could gather up, hold in my arms, and put on display. Then it struck me.

It's not what we achieve in our lives that validates us.

It's not what we're given—or even what we earn—that makes us important.

It's what we give to others that motivates us and makes life worth living.

Ultimately, I realized that a gift unshared is not a worthy gift. So I decided to start using my success in a way that benefited others. Over the years, people have sent me things to autograph, such as photos, helmets, footballs, and pennants. I've always just signed them and sent them back. But now I do something that benefits more than just the recipient of the signed item. Now, if you go to my website, JoeTheismann.com, you'll see a list of items with a dollar amount attached to them. Pick any item, and I'm happy to autograph it for you. All I ask for is a suggested donation. Every penny of your donation will go to St. Jude Children's Research Hospital.

I've found a small way to take some of the fruits of my labor and help others. I only wish that I had started doing that years ago. I was given certain abilities, and truthfully, I wasted them for many years; I was too busy seeking validation and feeding my ego. But I don't want to waste them anymore. And that's why a portion of the proceeds of this book will also go to St. Jude Children's Research Hospital.

It really is about helping others. That's the motivation that should get you moving in the morning. There's the importance of having pride in your work and yourself, the unmistakable warmth of a pat on the back, the sense of belonging, the sway of positive peer pressure, the appeal of competition, the need for validation, the power of fear—and of course, there's always the money. However, those rewards are all for *you*. I don't believe that life should be lived with such a narrow, selfish endgame.

What can you do to help someone else? When you achieve more success and start earning more money, what can that money do for others? When you excel at work and earn more freedom and more control over your time, what will you do with that time to enrich the lives of others?

Working hard so that I can use my time and talents to benefit the lives of others—that's the greatest motivator of all.

A friend asked me a few years ago if I thought I was a successful person. The question made me stop and think. I had spent fifteen years playing professional football and achieved some degree of success in my profession: Super Bowl Champion, league MVP, NFL Man of the Year, and so on. Yes, I considered my football career successful. I also spent twenty-three years broadcasting, and there was certainly a degree of success achieved in being able to be around that long. I have been speaking for close to forty years, allowing me to share my experiences in life with the people I engage with. I felt like I was a successful person, so I answered him, "Yes." He then began to explain to me that what I really did was have aspirations. I aspired to be a great football player; I aspired to, throughout my broadcasting, teach people about the game of football. Similarly, during my speeches, I aspire to share the stories and lessons in life I have learned to help people be better at what they want to accomplish. My friend then proceeded to explain to me the true definition of success. True success is when you have reached a point in life when you start giving back. Then, and only then, will you be truly successful.

To All You Champions Out There

Motivation isn't a science. It's an art form. As an artist, you mix together a little bit of this and a little bit of that to discover how to create a masterpiece. Once you settle on the right incentives that encourage you, use that formula to drive your goal-setting—and really, your life—to excellence.

But don't set goals in life that merely excite you; set goals that scare you a little bit. There's a quote often attributed to Eleanor Roosevelt that says, "Do something every day that scares you." If you do that, you'll strengthen your "motivation muscle." Find what motivates you, and then set your goals around it.

My goal is to change the lives of others by giving back and by sharing the wisdom passed down to me over the years. I realize it's an ambitious goal. But when we come together to change the world, the multiplier effect works its magic, and our actions—mine, yours, and everyone else's—combine to shake the very foundations upon which we stand.

What holds so many people back from achieving their goals is fear of failure—but if you don't take action, you'll fail by default. So what have you got to lose? Everyone has a different opinion on failure, and a lot of people have no tolerance for it. Yet failure is necessary (and even welcome) if it means that you learn what not to do, and then do it better the next time around.

The key is that when you do fail, you must do so quickly! Learn from those disappointments and make darn sure you don't make those mistakes again. Then, and only then, will those perceived failures have been worthwhile. I don't believe I've ever had a failure in my life. I've just had some "educational experiences" that didn't go my way.

And remember that you can have whatever you want in life, but nobody is going to give it to you. Everything of value must be earned. Decide right here and now that you are going to be a champion today. Decide that you are going to be a champion *every* day. Do it for yourself, for your company, for your family, and for all the other people in this world. You have the ability to touch their lives with your unique and special talents.

BONUS #6
Situational Success Isn't Always Enough

JOE WALTON WAS MY offensive coordinator in Washington for three years, and I credit him as the man who really taught me how to play the quarterback position. He was highly disciplined in the way he expected me to operate as a quarterback, and I discovered a great deal about becoming a meticulous and consistent player under his tutelage.

Joe was a real stickler for the disciplines of mechanizing my movements, like making my back foot hit first, then shuffling and throwing the same way every time. He also helped me learn the precise number of steps to take that coordinated with the routes that were being run—there was a three-step drop, a five-step drop, and a seven-step drop.

But Joe taught me a lot more than football mechanics. He also revealed to me a great lesson about "situational success." He taught me to not just accept my successes at face value, but to look at the situations and the circumstances behind each individual success.

Every week, I would meet one-on-one with Coach Walton to go over the previous week's game. During one of our meetings, after a game against the San Diego Chargers in 1980, I was feeling particularly good about my performance.

In the past, when we played the Chargers, Joe would always have at least three to four pages of corrections for me. This game was different. I had been on fire—I was 26 for 37 in completions, threw for 269 yards, and had 2 touchdown passes with no interceptions. I'd gone to bed that night thinking, *There's no way he's going to have pages of corrections this time. The game was too good.*

I soon discovered that I was sorely mistaken. As I sat down with Coach Walton, I found myself staring at three full pages of notes.

It was a deflating moment, to say the least. And my disappointment must have been written all over my face, because Coach Walton began explaining why I was staring at pages of notes after such a (in my mind anyway) phenomenal game. "Look, Joe," he said, "the game looked great on paper. You threw for almost three hundred yards; you had a ton of completions; you had two touchdown passes. But the defense you played against just isn't that good."

He continued, "As a matter of fact, you misread both of those touchdown passes, and if their defense had been where they were supposed to be, those passes would have been interceptions. I can't allow you to think that your mediocre performance was a great performance, because I want to prepare you to play against the best in the league, like the Dallas Cowboys and the New York Giants. If I allow you to think that your average performance was anything more than average, then when you play the *great* teams, you're not going to be up to the task."

Sometimes, when we think we've really done something special, we need to look at the situation in context to determine whether or not it is truly a success. If you defeat a five-year-old in a game of tennis, does that mean you are a great tennis player? If you're in sales, and a prospect says yes before you even begin your presentation, does that mean you are a great salesperson?

You're not a great tennis player because you beat a kindergartener, and you are not a great salesperson because a prospect was an easy sale. You're just lucky—and you just happened to be in the right place at the right time.

Situational success does not necessarily equate to greatness. Great performance in one situation may be nothing more than average in another.

When someone tells you *no*, he or she is actually saying, "I'm not sold yet. I need more information and more proof." With Coach Walton, I was an overly confident salesman who strutted in and said, "Look at what I've done. Joe Theismann is one great product, don't you think?"

In return, Coach Walton said, "Sorry, buddy. That performance didn't sell me on the product. I need you to look at the situation and the context in which you succeeded, and I need you to be better than what you thought you were. I need to prepare you to play against the best, so that you can be at your best."

We aren't always as good as we think we are. But champions decide that every day is a new day and a brand-new opportunity to "sell" others on why they are the best under *any* circumstances.

"What have you got to lose?

Right now is your 'someday' moment."

EXTRA POINT

A Letter to My Younger Self

THE FOLLOWING LETTER WAS first published in an online news-paper called *The Players' Tribune*, which was founded by Derek Jeter with the vision of being the "Voice of the Game." This is a letter that I wrote to my younger self, the Joey THEESMAN who once played pickup games back in South River, New Jersey.

If we could, I bet we would all send a message to our younger selves if it meant we could avoid some of the heartache and the trials that we knew were coming down the pike. But that's not the way life works, is it? We have to fall down. If we don't, we'll never discover what we're truly made of once we pick ourselves back up.

It was therapeutic to write these words to a fresh-faced Joe Theismann. As you read this letter, decide what advice you wish you could give to your younger self—and then take those words of wisdom and pass them along to your children, or to the next generation of champions.

DEAR JOE,

I already know how you're going to react to this. You're probably going to try to argue with every point I make here. Well, just read what I have to say and take my word for it.

First things first: On November 18, 1985, maybe take the night off (but more on that later).

I write you this letter on the night that you've learned that you finished runner-up for the Heisman Trophy. Even though it might feel like it right now, I can assure you that this is not the end of the world. You're going to reflect on your time at Notre Dame with a lot of pride and fond memories. You didn't win a trophy this time, but there might be a few waiting for you down the road.

Before your senior year, Notre Dame's PR director, Roger Valdiserri, convinced you to change the pronunciation of your last name so that it rhymes with the Heisman Trophy. From this experience, you'll learn a couple of things. First, voters aren't interested in gimmicks. Second, sometimes nicknames have a way of sticking. Say goodbye to Joe THEESMAN.

Whether you want to believe this or not, Joe, you don't know everything. Your hubris will make you attempt to navigate the draft process without the help of an agent. You're not as good at negotiating as you think you are. Your refusal to get a professional advisor will cause you to get emotionally involved in the business side of things, which will backfire on you.

I shouldn't have to tell you this, but maybe think twice about signing a contract with the Toronto Argonauts after you've already agreed to a contract with the Miami Dolphins. Coach Don Shula will rightfully rip you a new one for doing so. You can at least take solace in the fact that you will never again in your life have a grown man yell at you that much.

Looking back, you won't regret signing with Toronto—they simply made a better offer—but you'll always have a part of you that knows that Don Shula was the kind of coach who could have gotten the most out of you. He was a demanding, tough disciplinarian, which I wish you had the wisdom to realize is exactly what you need at this phase of your life.

If it makes you feel any better, Coach Shula will eventually stop hating you . . . in a few decades.

Playing for the Toronto Argonauts is going to be quite a jolt for you. You're going to learn that being a Heisman Trophy finalist doesn't mean squat north of the border. At first you'll wander the streets and think, "Wow, nobody here knows who I am—this is great!" But eventually this will turn into, "Wow, nobody here knows who I am—this is terrible." You might think that playing in Toronto is a humbling experience, but let me tell you now: You don't know anything about the word "humbled" yet, bud.

When you do come back stateside to play in the NFL, you'll have to start from the bottom of the barrel, grinding it out on special teams as a punt returner for a couple years. During this time, you'll also have the pleasure of sharing the quarterback meeting room with Billy Kilmer and Sonny Jurgensen, a couple of guys who hate your guts. Wait it out. You'll get your shot. And when you do, you're going to make it count.

You've always loved speed, and that will lead you to spend way too much money on a limited edition Corvette designed by John Greenwood. Pretty sweet ride, no? My advice is to save yourself some time and money by attaching a gigantic sign to your old car that says, "Hey, Officer, Please Give Me a Ticket!" You need to figure out what you need and eliminate what you don't. If you got money, keep money.

In 1981, a man named Joe Gibbs will come in to coach the team. Everyone, including you, will think your time is up in Washington. New coach, old quarterback—it'll seem like the writing is on the wall, particularly after the team starts the season with five losses. Here's some free advice: When you're not chosen by someone else, you better be really good at what you do because they'll look for any possible excuse to get rid of you. Don't give Coach Gibbs a reason to let you go because you still have your best football years ahead of you.

By 1985, all the accolades that you think make a man great will have been attained. NFL Man of the Year, MVP, and a Super Bowl trophy will all be yours. But what you're going to learn is that an entire life can change in one snap.

One night, you're going to get hurt. You're going to get hurt bad. And at that point, you're going to learn what's truly important in this life. People will call what happens to you a tragedy, but it really isn't. It's a blessing.

At the time, you'll have become so self-absorbed and wrapped up in your own celebrity that you won't think that you need anybody. But a rude awakening will come when you get out of that hospital with your leg in a cast and go to the Redskins training facility. When you get there, your locker of twelve years will be occupied by another player. All your personal items will be stashed away in a box in the equipment room. This world you had let consume you doesn't exist anymore.

Your emotional recovery will be much faster if you can come to terms with the fact that no amount of fame will give you joy if you can't respect yourself. Others may lead you to believe you hold some higher importance because of your exploits on the field, but that kind of fame is fleeting. Find value for yourself, Joe. Find value in what you do. Appreciate your work, and appreciate the people you work with, and don't expect any favors because it's just not going to happen.

You're going to learn that the only true currency is respect. If you learn to give it, you'll eventually get it.

I'll leave you with this: A few years after your career ends, you'll finally have a conversation about your injury with the man who caused it. You'll say to him, "We'll always be connected because of that play. You know how it affected my life, but how did it affect yours?"

And how he responds will always stick with you: "Joe, I learned a great lesson that night. No matter how great you are at what you do, it can be over in an instant. I ask people to snap their fingers to show them how quickly a life can change. I decided that night that I was going to make every snap—every single play in practice and during games—count. You might think you'll live forever, but you truly don't know when it's all going to be over, so don't leave anything on the table."

That's some pretty decent advice right there.

I'm proud of you.

ACKNOWLEDGMENTS

I would not have been able to write this book without the help and guidance of so many people.

My parents, who gave me a sound foundation to grow from and their love.

My coaches, teammates, and friends who were willing to share their insight and knowledge.

A special thanks to James Malinchak for his insistence that I "get off my butt and get it done."

Jennifer Lill Brown and Susan Canavan for their help with putting my thoughts into words.

Dann Moss and Dan Strone for finding the best choice for publishing my book, and to Scott Waxman, Mark Fretz, and Evan Phail of Radius Book Group for delivering beyond my vision. Without all of you, this book would not have happened.

And to my wife, Robin, for her patience and continued support to finish the project.

To my readers, I hope you've enjoyed this journey as much as I have. In this book, I've spoken often of my parents, and there is one thing that my dad always did that I hope will stay with you. He always gave a firm handshake and looked the other person in the eye.

I'm looking forward to shaking your hand the next time we meet.

—Joe